THE ART OF
TEA BAG
MANAGEMENT

How to Infuse a Revolution...

BY JEREMY BALL

The Art of Tea Bag Management

How to infuse a revolution

Jeremy Ball

Copyright © 2016 Jeremy Ball
All rights reserved.

ISBN: 1539816990
ISBN 13: 9781539816997
Library of Congress Control Number: 2016918210
CreateSpace Independent Publishing Platform
North Charleston, South Carolina

Preface

When I first decided to write this book, I chose not to start with the introduction but to go straight into writing the chapters. I had no idea why I did it, but something guided me. Upon completing all the other chapters, I returned to the final chapter, which in this case was the introduction. As a serendipitous twist of fate, it turned out that the week in which I was to write my introduction was also the same week in which we lost someone who, in my humble opinion, was the greatest leader of our generation: Nelson Mandela.

His death reminded me of just how great a leader he was and how he inspired much of what I share in this book. I had never really taken the time to look at who I have become or to see where some of my major life principles have come from. Now that I had just completed the chapters of my book and I had my thoughts down on paper for the first time, I was able to see these thoughts in a big-picture view. In doing so, I realized just how much of an influence Nelson Mandela has had on me.

Nelson Mandela had a never-ending commitment to wanting things to be better and to improving people's lives. He didn't hold on to past injustices; rather, he chose to focus on building a bright and better future for everyone, a philosophy known in South Africa as *ubuntu*, which—roughly translated—means "human kindness."

There are also other definitions of what ubuntu is, but for me, it is something profoundly simple and was described perfectly in a recent blog post by Sir Richard Branson, who asked a close aide and friend of Nelson Mandela's what it was that made Mandela such a great man. The aide responded, "He always does things for the good of the tribe." Although a simple response, it provided a profound insight into what drives such a great leader.

Ubuntu is about putting the good of the people first—being selfless instead of selfish. Most people understand this on a smaller scale, since most of us would do anything for the people we love. Ubuntu, however, suggests we do it for everyone.

I hope in some small way that this book inspires you and helps you apply the ubuntu philosophy within your own workplace. I also hope it will help you inspire the people around you to follow a similar path and help create a more sustainable and communal world for everyone. Divided we will fall, but united we will thrive.

While the loss of such a great man saddens me, it has served as a strong reminder to me about what is important in my life. I would therefore like to dedicate this book to the memory of Nelson Mandela and his unwavering desire to make the world a better place.

> **OUR TASK IS TO UNITE HUMANITY THROUGHOUT THE WORLD AND IF YOU ACT AS AN INDIVIDUAL, YOU WILL NEVER BE ABLE TO ACHIEVE THAT**
>
> -Nelson Mandela,
> Speaking at the first meeting of the Elders in 2007

Introduction

> **PEOPLE ARE OUR GREATEST ASSET**
>
> -Anonymous

This is one of the most common things you hear companies say, yet if you ask the people working for those companies how they feel, they will tell you something completely different.

While I believe the statement to be true—people are *any* company's most valuable asset—the problem with the statement is the use of the word *asset*. Companies make the mistake of seeing their people as assets rather than as people.

Like most things in life, theories can be taken out of context, and that is what I think happens here. People aren't assets; they *are* the company. Without people, a company is nothing, and the happier and more successful the people are, the happier and more successful the company will be.

In this book, I will teach you the art of tea bag management, a set of principles to create high-performing, inspired, and motivated people who not only work together to overcome challenges but also have a real passion for life and a desire to become the best they can be.

If you are anything like me, then there are two questions you are desperate to know the answers to before you read any further: *Who are you, and why should I believe what you say?*

Well, let's start with the first question. That's the easiest one to answer.

Who Am I?

By now, you know that my name is Jeremy Ball. I was born in England on July 29, 1970, and I am the youngest of four boys.

The United Kingdom went through a very difficult time in the seventies. The economy was struggling, and opportunities were limited, especially for a young family with four children. Because of the lack of opportunities in Britain, my parents decided to look abroad to provide a better life for our family. In 1976, they decided to sell everything they had, and in July of that year, we went to South Africa on a three-week vacation with the intention to stay. My parents had friends who had already emigrated and whom my father had been over to see previously, but this was a chance for my mother to see if she would like it. She did.

I can't imagine how difficult a decision it must have been for my parents to move to a new country with four young children, aged between five and ten, leaving behind all their family and friends in order to give us a better life with more opportunities. It was an extremely brave decision and one for which I am eternally grateful.

Growing up in apartheid South Africa afforded me a unique upbringing. My father worked on the construction of Sasol II, a large petrochemical plant in a predominantly Afrikaans area. At the time, I had no understanding of what apartheid was, but as an English kid growing up in an Afrikaans town, I learned firsthand about discrimination and how it felt to be both the oppressor and the oppressed.

As a white person, I benefited from all the privileges that having the "right" skin color provided me, but as an English kid, I was subject to the anger of the Afrikaans because of the British government's opposition to the apartheid state. My friends and I tried to avoid fights—sometimes unsuccessfully—that erupted among us because of our nationalities.

It was difficult to understand because, apart from nationality and language, there was no real difference between me and the Afrikaans children. We all liked sports, music, and having fun with our friends, but because of the political situation, I was "the English kid," and that meant we were foes.

In 2002, I returned to the United Kingdom, and what I encountered was both unexpected and ironic. After twenty-seven years of being called "the English kid" in South Africa, I was now being referred to as "the South African guy" to all my colleagues in the office. Instead of feeling as if I belonged in the country of my birth, once again, I felt like an outsider. Because I had learned to live with this feeling in South Africa, I didn't mind it too much, but it did surprise me. It made me realize how greatly people feel the need to put others into boxes and give them labels. I guess it makes some people feel safer to categorize others.

Truth be told, I don't feel like I am English or South African; I feel a loyalty to both countries, but I don't feel like either defines who I am.

Coming back to Britain allowed me to do a lot of traveling. I'd always wanted to travel, but with South Africa being so far away from the main transport routes, travel was both time-consuming and expensive. In the first job I had when I returned to Britain, I worked nine-day fortnight, which meant that I had every second Friday off. I took full advantage of this and used the three-day weekends as opportunities to travel around Britain and Europe. I even managed to fit in a couple of trips to New York.

During these traveling adventures, I started to realize how similar people were. Growing up in South Africa, my brother Julian would tell me, "Any money spent on travel is money well spent because travel broadens the mind." And just as he had foretold, traveling was an eye-opening experience, exposing me to many different beliefs, points of view, and cultural norms.

One of the things that stood out for me was that no matter where I went, regardless of the political, religious, or cultural differences, people acted very similarly in given situations. If the place I visited had an aggressive atmosphere, the people would act aggressively. Similarly, if the atmosphere was jubilant and festive, then the people would be jubilant and festive. Their responses seemed to have more to do with the environment than their nationality or culture.

Today, traveling is still one of my favorite hobbies. Over the past ten years, I have had some wonderful experiences, been to some amazing places, and met some incredible people. I am still in contact with many of these people and have become good friends with them. My passion for traveling, my curiosity for life, and my interest in people have kept me on my path. My travels have taught me that under all the conditioning and protective layers, people are intrinsically good. They believe that the world is a good place.

Why Should You Believe Me?

This is probably going to sound strange, but I don't think you should believe me. I don't say that because I think what I have to say is not important; on the contrary, I think the principles are very important. In fact, I think they should be taught in school. I say this because I want you to try these principles for yourself, not simply believe them and then put this book on a shelf.

I had been applying these principles for a number of years without realizing the power in what I was doing. It was only recently, after I had completed another successful assignment that had achieved fantastic results, that I felt the need to analyze and document it. On two previous assignments, I had been frustrated because I had achieved so much, only to see things return to the way they had been after I had departed. This book is the result of that analysis, and it details the process I had been using. Now you can use my process and principles to achieve the same results.

I know there are many people out there who claim to have found the answer, and if anyone tells you that, my advice would be to run as far away as you can. In my experience, learning is a journey, and to truly learn something, you have to apply the knowledge. Knowledge is power, but only if you use it. This is why I want you to take these principles and apply them yourself—because until you have, you will never fully understand them. I want you to become curious about the possibilities and make your own conclusions. There is no one true way in life, just a multitude of possible outcomes, and by learning and applying, you can see for yourself what works and what doesn't.

Navigating through This Book

When I first decided to write this book, I only intended to cover the three parts involved in implementing the art of tea bag management.

However, my partner pointed out to me that much of the success I achieved in applying the principles had a lot to do with who I was as a person and all the personal and interpersonal skills I had learned along the way—all of which can be learned by you and are detailed in this book.

After becoming aware of this, I decided to create the book in two parts. The first part focuses on you, the individual, the person who is ultimately responsible for implementing the principles outlined in the following chapters. Part two focuses on the implementation of these principles and details the various pieces required to put them in place.

People often ask me what tea bag management is and how I came up with the title. The concept originated with a metaphor I created to explain how my style of management works. Because so much of my process is invisible to the naked eye, people could see the great results I was getting, but they couldn't see or even understand *how* I was getting them.

I remember sitting in my office and trying to explain it to one of my colleagues without much success. We decided to take a break and get a drink. He got a coffee, and I got my usual rooibos tea. I poured the water in the cup and then put the tea bag in. We made our way back to the office, and as I put the cup on the table, I saw the flavor of the tea bag infusing the water. I showed this to him, and—straightaway—he could visualize what I was talking about.

I explained to him that there are three key parts. The first is the cup, which symbolized my area of responsibility. Everything inside the cup was my responsibility; I was responsible for what went in and what came out. So whatever happened inside the cup was mine to deal with—no one else's.

The water symbolized the environment and culture within my area of responsibility. As you know, water is the key ingredient to creating all forms of life; without water, there is no life. It is the first thing that scientists look for when looking for life on other planets, because they know that wherever there is water, there is a chance of life. In my metaphor, the water symbolized my desire to create an environment that encouraged people to live and grow. And while that may seem a little dramatic, one of my greatest desires as a manager is to inspire the people I have the privilege and honor to manage to live more passionate lives and become the best people they can be. It is therefore critical that the "water" facilitates that.

The third and final part is the tea bag, which symbolized me, the manager or leader. As the authority, once I have immersed myself into the environment, my essence (personality, habits, beliefs, and characteristics) will naturally infuse into the surrounding water. Whether I like it or not, I *will* affect the people under my responsibility. It is therefore up to me whether I want to influence them in a positive or a negative way. This principle applies to both professional and personal lives.

Of course, there is much more involved, but this metaphor clearly shows the three main factors. One key distinction is that your power to influence is directly proportional to the amount of certainty and confidence you have. In any situation, the most confident person will generally hold the greatest power to influence.

This book contains six chapters, each containing a key principle. To help you remember the six key principles, I use the following mnemonic:

> T > E > A > C > U > P >

Each letter links to one of the six chapter titles:

The mnemonic can also be split for the two parts of the book. Part one, which focuses specifically on the manager and is symbolized by the tea bag in the main metaphor, is

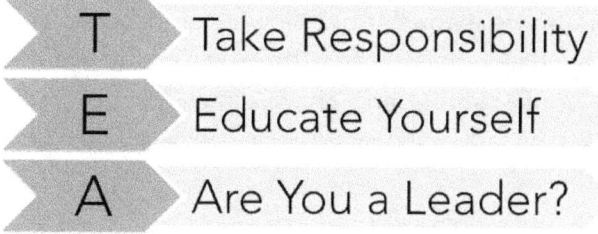

And part two, which focuses on the actual implementation, is

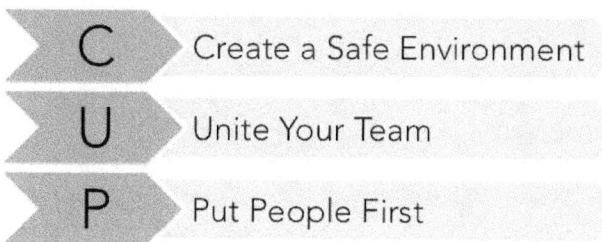

As you progress through the book, I use the mnemonic throughout the chapter to remind you of where you are in the process.

While part one is not directly involved in the implementation, it is an integral part in the whole process, as it contains some key skills and character traits that will help you throughout the implementation process. It is worth noting that the information and skills discussed in part one do not form a completely conclusive list of all the management skills that would benefit you, and I suggest you continue to develop your skills beyond the areas covered.

Closing

I know you will find a lot of value in this book, and I am extremely grateful for your decision to purchase it. If we are to reach anywhere close to the amazing potential we have as a people on this planet, we are going to need as many people as we can get to champion the cause and start being more caring to one another. Throughout the book, I remind you that great leaders create more leaders, not followers, and I hope you will step up and accept the challenge. We have the potential to achieve so much—but only if we work together and change the direction in which we are headed.

Take Responsibility

Everything Starts with You

The Hardest Lesson

For many people, this is the hardest lesson they will ever have to learn but probably one of the most valuable. However, if you get this lesson—if you truly understand that everything starts with you—then for the first time in your life, you will have the option of gaining control of it.

I am the first to admit that it is not an easy lesson to learn, and there are still times when I forget. It is so difficult for us, as adults, to know where our conditioning actually comes from. The first seven years of our lives comprise the period that psychologists call the "imprint period," when children's brains are like sponges. The senses capture billions of bits of information per second and stream them straight into the subconscious brain. At that early age, there is very little filtering, so everything we see gets absorbed. We are not very mobile, so we have to rely on others to move us around. Those early years are very curious years. We start to understand our senses and develop a picture of our physical environment.

Between the ages of seven and fourteen, we enter the next phase of our development, commonly known as the "modeling" phase. The modeling phase is the phase sociologists believe is responsible for defining generations. By that they mean that the major social issues a child is exposed to during those years tend to be the main factors in defining a child's views as an adult. During the modeling phase, children develop their perceptions of their physical realities and start to develop their social realities by modeling their parents. While events continue to condition us throughout our lives, it is during this phase that social conditioning is most influential.

While at this age we are quite mobile, our parents limit our access to the outside world. They are our prime models of the world, and as a result, we inherit many of their conditioned beliefs. The major issues that affect the family during this period play significant roles in children's adult lives. Religion, political views, favorite sports teams, and even our favorite foods are infused into us during the modeling period.

Around the age of fifteen, we move into a new phase commonly known as the "socializing" period, which comprises a large part of our teenage years and is when we first start to experience freedom. We are still living at home with our parents, but we are old enough to venture out of the house without our parents' full protection.

During the socializing period, we start to find new models in the world. These can come in the form of movie stars, rock stars, cartoon heroes, friends, parents of friends, and other popular figures of the time.

For most of us, it is these three phases in which we get conditioned by others without any real filtering because we see the various role models as authorities. We take their words as gospel.

Conditioning is a natural occurrence, and there is nothing wrong with it, but it is extremely valuable to acknowledge that conditioning does exist and that many of the things we do, believe, or say come down to our conditioning.

The great thing is that our conditioning is not permanent and can be undone. All it takes is our willingness to change and some effort to do so.

If you have acknowledged that everything starts with you, then you have taken a big step forward to learning the hardest lesson.

Feel the Fear

One of the most common things that conditioning has given us is a condition to blame others for our problems. Because so few of us ever learn the hardest lesson, we are very quick to blame those around us for things that happen to us, even if it had nothing at all to do with them. In the book *Feel the Fear and Do It Anyway* by Susan Jeffers, she explains that everything that happens to you is your responsibility.

When I first read this, I struggled to get my head around the concept. How could it be that if I was late for a meeting because I was stuck in traffic on the way there, my being late was my fault? Surely, it was the traffic's fault I was late. But, according to Suzanne, "I chose to take that route; I also chose to leave at that time; therefore it was my responsibility." I had complete control of both decisions, and while I had no idea the traffic would be that bad, I had chosen to leave at that time and take that route.

The underlying message is that until you accept responsibility for everything that happens to you, you will be a victim. A victim of time, of other people's actions, of the weather, the traffic, and all the other things you choose to blame. This concept is not about blame or fault, but about taking responsibility—your ability to respond.

The Art of Tea Bag Management

The irony of it is you can never be in complete control of your life if you allow yourself to be a victim. By choosing to be a victim, you unwittingly give away your control and your ability to change any given situation.

One of the common attributes of all great leaders is that they take full responsibility for everything that happens to them. No matter how unpredictable circumstances can be, they still acknowledge that the decisions they alone made resulted in what happened to them. They realize that, without taking responsibility, they would be unable to change the situation, and that would mean they were powerless.

In order for you to get the results you want from this book, you have to understand this essential point, because unless you do, you will look to blame your team for things that happen in your area of responsibility. By blaming your team, you hand over your control to them and lose your status as leader—not to mention, you create less-than-ideal working conditions and levels of trust.

No one said being a leader was going to be easy. It takes a willingness to learn and break down any nonserving belief structures. The road of self-discovery and inner mastery can be a long, lonely road, but it is essential if you truly want to be a great leader.

Change Comes from Within

The world is full of different belief systems, cultures, and religions. The one thing they all seem to agree on is that change comes from within. As hard as this may be to understand, the world around us is simply a projection of who we are at this moment in time. The clothes we wear, the foods we eat, the cars we drive—they are all representative of who we are at this moment in time. The choices we make create the world we have around us. Some of the choices we make we don't even realize we

are making. They are part of our unconscious conditioning, and we make them on autopilot.

In modern society, we rarely take the time to actually contemplate what is happening around us—to truly stop and think about the things we do or say. We blindly go through our day believing that we *go out into the world* rather than knowing that we *create our world*.

So much about reality is based on our perceptions of things. Even the idea of truth is a perception of what we believe. Imagine, for example, that you go to watch a ball game with your best friend. You both support different teams, but you choose to sit next to each other. If during the game, a ref makes a controversial call and your friend's team ends up winning the game, you will both have seen exactly the same game but will walk away with two completely different realities. You will obviously feel aggrieved that the decision didn't go your way, but your friend will justify the decision. At that moment, you have chosen to see the world differently from your friend, and without knowing it, the decisions you make will be affected by your perception.

Our unconscious minds are constantly making decisions based on our beliefs of what is right and wrong, beliefs we inherited thanks to our conditioning.

When you leave the ball game, it is highly unlikely that you will be making empowered decisions. You might decide to stop at the bar and have a couple of drinks to drown your sorrows. After a few too many drinks, you may decide to stop and get a burger from a fast-food joint on the way home. The next morning, you wake up with a hangover and feel a little sick, so you decide not to go to work. When you go to the office the following day, you find out that you have been fired. All of a sudden, the world seems like a very unfair place.

The Art of Tea Bag Management

The lack of income caused by your losing your job will affect the type of clothes you buy, the food you eat, and the car you drive. While this may all sound a little extreme, these kinds of patterns are happening all the time without your even knowing. In this example, it could have all turned out differently if you had made a decision not to feel aggrieved by the referee's decision. That simple choice could have changed the entire sequence of events, and the choice to change that decision would be yours.

In every moment, you have the power to make a decision. Sure, in some situations you may feel you have a lot of choices while in others you may feel you have none. However, at some stage leading up to the place where you had no perceived choice, you had a choice to make a decision that would not have left you in that place.

In life, you have to make some tough decisions, and you may not always make the right ones, but you will always have a choice. If you want to change your life or your world, you have to start from within, and that starts with taking responsibility for the decisions you make—good or bad.

Where Is Your Control?

As a leader, understanding why we do the things we do and say the things we say is vitally important because many of the things we do in our daily routines are done unconsciously. In this section of the book, I examine that element of control in more detail. Remember, of course, the previous section—everything starts from within.

Internal versus External Locus of Control

"Locus of control" is a theory first developed in 1954 by Julian B. Rotter. Certain aspects of personality studies now commonly use this theory.

The theory suggests there are two loci of control, either internal or external. The idea of an internal locus of control suggests that individuals accept full responsibility for all the decisions they make. The external locus of control suggests individuals accept no responsibility for the decisions they make.

As an example, let's imagine you're taking a driving test. The driving test doesn't go too well, so you fail the test. If you are operating from an internal locus of control, you might put the failure down to the fact that you have not prepared properly and vow to go away and practice until you feel confident enough to retake the test. However, if you are operating from an external locus of control, you might put the failure down to external factors like the car not being like the one you are used to or that the driving instructor just didn't like you. You might leave the testing ground feeling aggrieved and tell all your friends how you have been wronged. Chances are, you won't feel you need to do any additional preparation, and you will just rebook your test, hoping you get a better car and nicer instructor.

In the example above, you would be far more likely to succeed in passing your driver's test if you were operating from an internal locus of control because when you retake the test you will be much better prepared.

There have been numerous studies carried out to test this theory. These studies support the idea that people who operate from an internal locus of control constantly achieve greater results than those operating from an external locus of control.

The diagram below is a visual representation of an internal-locus-of-control principle, with the circle representing you.

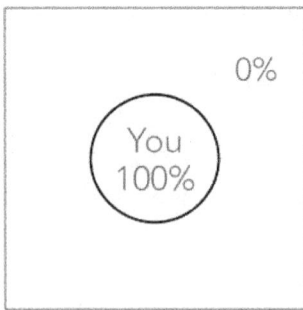

You can only ever truly control yourself, and therefore, 100 percent of control exists inside the circle. While you may be able to influence things outside of the circle, you never really have the ability to control any of it.

Transitioning from an external locus of control to an internal locus of control is not easy—it's going to take effort. It won't happen overnight, and it will take a lot of practice to master it, but for any budding leader, it is essential you do. It is a key factor required in order to master the art of tea bag management.

You Can't Control People

There may be some people who disagree that you can't control other people, and they would be right. All over the world, people are being

controlled. Some of them allow themselves to be controlled, and others are controlled by force.

What you need to consider, though, is that whatever or whoever is controlling them has to continually maintain that control over their subjects. Take a look at the prison system, for example. The prison wardens have to work constantly to prevent the inmates from escaping. They use state-of-the-art surveillance equipment; safe, secure buildings; and, when necessary, they exert extreme force. You could say, then, that the inmates are being controlled, and—thankfully, in most cases—they are controlled successfully.

But what would happen if the surveillance equipment was turned off, the building left insecure, and the prison wardens not present? Do you think the inmates would remain inside the prison?

One of the biggest mistakes most managers make is attempting to control people by giving them strict rules to follow. While they will get results, the only reason is because of constantly imposing these controls. If, for whatever reason, controls are removed, those manager no longer get the same results. This type of control severely affects a manager's ability to leave people to work unattended. As soon as they turn their back or disappear from the situation, it is very likely that people will stop working the way the manager would want them to.

I can demonstrate this point by inflating a balloon. The balloon represents your area of control. As you blow into the balloon, it will inflate until you decide it is big enough for the purpose you require. Now you have to keep your fingers closed over the hole you used to inflate the balloon. As soon as you remove your fingers, the air will escape from the balloon. The air will only remain in the balloon if you force it to remain there.

This ongoing need to maintain force to control the situation creates stress, tension, and pressure. As a manager, you are constantly concerned

The Art of Tea Bag Management

about the air escaping from the balloon and would need to impose other controls, like tying a knot in the end of the balloon, to make sure this doesn't happen. This will have the desired effect in the short-term; however, the air will eventually escape, and you will need to reinflate the balloon. Life is constantly looking for equilibrium, and as soon as you apply any kind of pressure, life will seek out balance and find a way to release the pressure.

The air in the balloon isn't really trying to go anywhere; it's just fighting against the pressure being applied to it. If I had not blown air into the balloon in the first place, there would be no need for the air to want to escape.

The trick, which I explain later, is to have your people want to be there without your having to impose any controls.

You Can Control Your Environment

While in the previous section I explained why I believe you can't control people, in this section, my aim is to show you how—by having control of the environment where people are—you are able to influence them.

Having lived in different countries all my life, I know firsthand just how much power the environment you live in can have on you. When I was about nineteen and living in South Africa, my parents moved to a little town called Mossel Bay on the Western Cape coast. It was the first time in my life I had lived near the coast.

At the time, the town was quite small, but it was situated on a beautiful bay, making it a great place to live. Scuba diving was a very popular activity with the friends I had met, so it wasn't long before I, too, took up scuba diving. I had always loved the idea of scuba diving, but it had never been a lifelong dream of mine. I started scuba diving largely because the environment was conducive to it, so it was an easy thing to do. I am very glad I did, too, because I ended up loving it and still do today.

A couple of years later, I moved on to the city of Durban. Durban is one of South Africa's main cities and is in the KwaZulu-Natal province on the east coast of South Africa. The seas on the east coast of South Africa are much warmer because of the warm Agulhas current that comes down from the east coast of Africa. Durban, unlike Mossel Bay, is not as popular for diving, as the sea is far more turbulent. The turbulent sea and currents reduce the visibility, so most dive spots tend to be further off the coast and accessed by boat.

What Durban lacked in diving, however, it made up for with its surfing. The turbulent sea; long, sandy beaches; and tourist piers make Durban an ideal place for surfing. Most of the friends I met when I moved to Durban were surfers. So just like I did in Mossel Bay, without anyone forcing me, I took up a new activity; this time it was surfing.

The Art of Tea Bag Management

In both these situations, I adapted to the environments without any peer pressure. Just spending time talking and listening to my friends was enough to make me want to join in. At the time, I didn't questions things as I do now, so I didn't realize what was happening. As I look back, however, I can see just how much of an impact the environment had on me.

When I was first given responsibility for a team at work, I had no plan of how I wanted to do things. I just did what came naturally to me. It was only when I looked back to try to understand why my leadership style was proving so successful that I was able to notice certain characteristics and traits I possessed that were different from my past managers'—things I was doing naturally that would otherwise have passed by without notice.

Now I see examples of this powerful principle in many different areas of life. The simple act of filling an ice cube tray with water and putting it in the freezer to make ice demonstrates this principle. At no stage are you making the water turn into ice; you are merely putting it in an environment that is conducive to making ice. If you merely left the water outside the freezer, it would not change, as the environment outside the freezer is not conducive to making ice.

For me, the environment is a critical ingredient for the development of a high-performing, motivated team. And the leader has the power to decide what the environment will be. While many of the principles I talk about in this book focus on the business aspect, they can be applied to every area of life.

The Path of Meaning

From the day we are born, we are constantly trying to attach meaning to the things we experience. During the imprint period, much of a child's time is spent trying to figure out what all the information they are receiving means. With no prior experiences to call on, a child looks to their parents for guidance. In this section, I look into *meaning* in more detail, so we can better understand what comprises a meaning.

How Do You Choose Meaning?

Have you ever wondered why you react to things in a certain way or why people react differently to a similar situation? While there are many factors that influence the way we act, including social proof and the environment, one of the major internal influences is meaning.

We are constantly giving meaning to things we experience, and these meanings influence how we behave. Meanings, like beliefs, are subconscious patterns we have developed throughout our lives. In neuro-linguistic programming (NLP), meanings are often referred to as *complex equivalences*.

Complex equivalences may not make any logical sense to anyone but the individual themselves because of the large number of factors that may be involved. But all too often in today's society, people criticize one another based on the meanings they themselves place on things, rather than trying to understand what it means to the other person.

> **NEVER CRITICIZE A MAN UNTIL YOU'VE WALKED A MILE IN HIS MOCCASINS**
> -Native American Proverb

Until we truly understand all the factors that collide to create a meaning, it is very difficult to comment on someone else's reactions.

Complex equivalences combine seemingly unrelated factors to create meaning. I recall reading a story in which a young boy noticed that his mother was feeling really sad. She was a single mother and had been feeling the strain of bringing up the young boy alone. The boy knew his mother loved white flowers, so in order to try to cheer her up, he went into the neighbor's yard and picked some flowers to give to her. The young boy returned home full of excitement and joy, with a lovely bunch of flowers in his hand. He told his mother how much he loved her and gave her the flowers. His mother, however, recognized the flowers from her neighbor's yard and began shouting at the boy. She told him how naughty he was and sent him to his room. The boy sat in his room, confused by what had just happened, and finally arrived at the conclusion that flowers are bad and make people sad.

As an adult, the boy received criticism from his partner for not showing his affections by giving flowers. The memories of the experience he had of his mother may have long since faded, but the meaning he had given to flowers remained.

Just like the conditioning mentioned earlier, we can change meanings once we are aware they exist. A good leader understands the complexity of meanings and seeks to understand other people before making any judgment on things they do or say.

The Cycle of Meaning

Some say that the quality of our lives is found in one element: our ability to choose the meaning in any life circumstance. It is the meaning we give to things that decides how we react to them.

TEACUP

Understanding meaning is an extremely valuable skill to learn, as meaning plays a significant role in the results we achieve in life, both good and bad. And this can be understood by the cycle of meaning shown below.

The cycle of meaning suggests that once we have given meaning to an event, the type of meaning we give that event will result in our experiencing an emotion. The emotion we feel affects the action we take. And the action we take in response to that emotion has a certain result.

Imagine, for example, that you are sitting at home on your couch, watching TV. Out of the corner of your eye, you notice a spider crawling up the wall. If you consider spiders to be friendly and don't mind spiders living in your house, the meaning you give to the spider crawling up the wall would be that it's OK. This wouldn't stir up any kind of emotion, and you would probably just go back to watching TV without doing anything about it. This would result in you enjoying your TV show. The spider would continue on its way.

But if you were scared of spiders and saw the spider crawling up the wall, that would probably mean a bad thing and stir up feelings of fear. Now, depending on the intensity of that feeling, you would probably try to capture it in a glass or jar and place it outside the house or simply kill it. Getting rid of the spider would then make you feel a little more relaxed.

Whenever we place a meaning on something, it causes a response and, ultimately, a result. By being aware of the meanings we attach to things, we can control the outcomes we achieve. We can also use this principle to help those in our team to achieve different results by finding out the meanings they attach to things. To get a different result, you can try to change the meaning. A great way to do this is by reframing the things to which they have attached meanings.

The Three Elements That Influence Meaning

Now that we have a better understanding of how meanings affect us, we will take a more detailed look into three major elements that influence our meanings. Understanding how each contributes will help you deconstruct yours or those of your team.

The first are the more tangible or physical aspects and include the following:

* Physiology
* Focus
* Language

These three aspects allow you to see immediately how people react to things. If, for example, you are out with friends and mention something that one person in the group finds sad, you would immediately see that friend's physiology change. Your friend's head would drop; their shoulders would roll forward, and more than likely, your friend would start to stare toward the ground.

This type of physiology is typical of people who are feeling down, sad, or depressed. While there is so much more behind people's meanings, these three body elements give you the earliest signs of what is going on with them. They are also the first three things you should focus on when trying to get somebody out of that state. Help them reframe the meaning they have applied to a given situation.

In the example used above, the best way to get your friend out of that state would be, first, to reassure your friend that everything is OK. Then, find a way to change your friend's physiology. Get your friend to stand up or to walk around. Once you get your friend to change their physiology, you would then try to change the focus. You do this by changing the language you use to more upbeat, friendly, or happy language and helping your friend focus on something else. You could also use language to ask your friend empowering questions that also serve to change their focus.

Obviously, depending on the particular situation you are dealing with, you have to be sensitive, but always look to address all three of the body elements. This of course also applies when dealing with your own emotional states.

The subsequent elements are far less obvious to notice than the previous because these are nontangible and happen at an unconscious level. They are hardwired into each of us but differ for each person and will affect how each person responds to situations. According to human-needs psychology, a branch of psychology I focus on in the next chapter of this book, these nontangible elements can be broken down into three main forces:

1. Driving force
2. Guiding force
3. Fuel of choice (emotions)

Driving force is comprised of a mix of six human needs and two primal fears. They exist in everybody but not always in the same quantities.

The guiding force is best described as our own personal beliefs and therefore is not necessarily present in everyone. Our guiding force is comprised of things like our:

* rules for life,
* global beliefs,

The Art of Tea Bag Management

* religious beliefs,
* identity, and
* values.

Our personal beliefs are largely influenced by our conditioning and environment. They can be vastly different from one person to the next.

The last force to consider is the fuel of choice, more commonly known as our emotions. Emotions are extremely powerful and should be handled with sensitivity. When the emotional brain is activated, the logical brain gets overrun. The emotional brain acts at a primary level because one of its prime functions is to keep you safe. However, not all emotions are beneficial, so developing a level of control over your emotions is a key skill for any leader. As a leader, those around you will look to you for guidance in stressful situations, so how you respond will influence how those around you respond.

To give you an example, imagine a parent and a child are having a picnic. They sit on a blanket and enjoy their freshly made sandwiches and cold drinks when a bee is attracted to the cold drinks and flies over. If this is the first time the child has experienced a bee, and the parent displays fear, the child will see the fear and become scared. There is a good chance the child will then make an association that bees are dangerous and carry that fear into adult life. However, had the parent remained calm and made the child feel safe, the child would not associate any fear with the bee.

These unconscious patterns and habits are running within us all the time and being passed down from generation to generation without our even being aware of them. It is only when we start to look for these patterns that we can change them.

Throughout this chapter, I have discussed the importance of taking responsibility and how the decisions we make and the actions we take create the world around us, whether we are aware of them or not. We looked at how any change has to start from within and that, if we want something to change, we have to initiate the change. We also touched on how the environments we are in affect us and that we can create useful environments to instigate a change. Finally, I discussed how the meanings we attach to things make us act in certain ways.

As leaders, it is crucial we take responsibility for everything that happens in our lives; otherwise, we allow ourselves to be affected by the situations and people around us.

In the next chapter, I look at the importance of learning new skills, and I discuss ideas on how to create a learning state that encourages you to learn. I also discuss two key skills I believe are fundamental for anyone aspiring to be a great leader.

Educate Yourself

There was a time during my school career when even the thought of having to educate myself made me anxious; I had a real love-hate relationship with school. I loved learning, but being a curious, creative person in a conservative school system with its rigid teaching style and pro-apartheid syllabus didn't work for me.

I wanted to know how things worked, and if I didn't understand, I would ask. I pick up concepts quickly, and if I get curious about something, I have an urge to know more, so I ask a lot of questions. For some teachers, though, it was more convenient if students just accepted what they said, especially when the subject they were teaching was based on little or no factual evidence.

By the time I reached my final year in school, I had lost all interest in education. Education, to me, involved my having to memorize what somebody else thought was important. There was little or no room for discussion or an alternative point of view. Either I repeated what I had been taught word-for-word, or I wasn't considered very clever and was treated like an outcast.

These days, however, things have changed. The Internet has revolutionized our access to information. Information that in my day was impossible to access is now accessible on a mobile phone. I first realized what a powerful resource the Internet can be for learning in 2005. At the time, I was stuck in a bit of a rut. Even though I had a job I liked, had purchased my first property (albeit with lodgers to help pay the mortgage), and was doing a lot of traveling with trips to Europe or North America once a month, something was missing. I felt like I had more to give, that there was so much more I could be doing with my life.

I remember kneeling at the end of my bed. It was Friday, March 4, 2005, at about seven in the evening, and I had my laptop open with Google ready in front of me on the bed. I had just been on the phone with one of my friends who'd called to see how I was doing. Something was churning inside me; I was sad and depressed about this missing thing, and I didn't know what to do. I had so many questions I wanted answered, but no one around could help me. I felt helpless and trapped, and out of pure frustration, I typed my question into Google and hit the Enter key. Before the computer had a chance to respond, I dropped my head down in resignation. After a couple of minutes, I lifted my head in mild curiosity to look at my computer. The screen was full of search results containing the answers I was looking for. It was such a pivotal moment in my life that I still remember it vividly. I instantly filled up with curiosity and hope, as if I had found a lost treasure chest.

It probably sounds crazy that I wouldn't think to use the Internet to find information on subjects that I was interested in, but until that point it had never occurred to me. Of course, I used the Internet for the typical things one would look for, such as booking my travel arrangements and looking for things I needed to buy. But seventeen years after leaving school, I had finally found a way to learn that suited me, and I grasped it

The Art of Tea Bag Management

with open arms. Today I use the Internet all the time and am constantly learning new skills.

In this chapter, I share with you some of the most powerful things I have learned to date. Not only will they help you become a great leader, but also—in my opinion—they will make every area of your life better.

The Learning State

When I look back at my school career, one thing that always surprises me is how fearful the environment was. There were so many rules and punishments for getting things wrong that most people were afraid to try. We were constantly being tested and told how difficult the final exams would be if we didn't study hard and do well on the tests.

The problem with a fear-based approach is that when feeling afraid, we react from the amygdala, a structure located within the older, reptilian part of the brain that is dominated by survival instincts. When active, the amygdala scans the environment for any danger, compromising logical and creative thinking with rigid and repetitive patterns. This often results in reactive fight or flight behavior, which isn't conducive to learning.

In this next section, I cover tips and tools to help you get the most out of the learning process, and I detail two powerful ingredients needed to create a successful learning state.

Be Curious

The first ingredient is curiosity. As I mentioned earlier in this section, the Internet has revolutionized learning. There is an almost unlimited supply of information available to anyone who wants it. All you have to do is enter your search query into your favorite browser and wait to see what comes back.

In my opinion, all learning starts with being curious about a subject. Curiosity is the seed that, when planted, will take on a life of its own. If you are curious, you will find what you're looking for because there is excitement in being curious that will drive you, even when you don't feel like you are getting results. In fact, the only thing that will stop you is when the effort you need to source the information is greater than your curiosity for the answers you seek.

The Art of Tea Bag Management

In every one of us, there is an inherent desire to want to learn and grow. It is part of our evolutionary makeup because we are hardwired to evolve. It is learning that enables us to adapt to our environment and evolve as a species.

If you look at the great leaders throughout history, they all shared a common desire to learn. They constantly sought new information to empower themselves and figure out how things within their environment worked. It is where the old adage "knowledge is power" originated.

In today's world, learning has never been easier, with so many great resources available at the touch of a button. We have unlimited resources like TED.com (the nonprofit conference video site dedicated to "ideas worth spreading") and YouTube, which are free to use and full of great content.

Curiosity is the key to unlocking information and is beautifully explained by the "hole-in-the-wall" experiment carried out by Professor Sugata Mitra in 1999. For the experiment, Professor Mitra placed a computer in a kiosk in a rural village in India. He made a hole in the wall to allow the children access the computer that sat behind a screen, but he didn't leave any instructions on what they were to do with the computer. Over a period of a few months, armed with nothing more than curiosity and a mouse that they could control, the children taught themselves how to use the computer and how to use the Internet to get information. What was even more remarkable was that many of the children couldn't even speak English, yet the computer only had English.

Because of the success of the initial experiment, Professor Mitra went on to replicate the experiment a number of times and has now won numerous awards for his research in education. His work epitomizes the importance of curiosity for learning.

As you continue to learn valuable leadership skills, your curiosity will drive you.

Enjoy Learning

The second key ingredient in learning is enjoyment. In the introduction to this chapter, I touched on the role the amygdala plays in the traditional school environment: stifling creativity and restricting logic. Even though things are changing, it pays to be aware of how you view learning.

In the previous chapter, we looked at how the three key phases in our development—the imprint period, the modeling period, and the socializing period—play a big part in our conditioning. It is therefore valuable to note that your school career overlaps all three of these key phases, and there are people who believe that was done deliberately in order to gain greater control of society.

As you know, school was not a great place for me to learn and put me off so much that I chose not to go to college or university, choosing instead to go straight to work. It was only when I discovered the power of the Internet as a learning tool in 2005 that I rekindled my love for learning. While my drive to learn at the time was from desperation, not love, during that process, I broke my old perception of learning that I had gained from my school days.

When I started to apply what I was learning and—even better—got results, it almost turned into a game. I would become curious about something, do research on and learn a certain aspect of the subject, take what I had learned, apply what I had learned in a real-world situation, and test the feedback. It made it fun and enjoyable, and the more successes I achieved, the more I enjoyed it—creating a positive feedback loop.

The Art of Tea Bag Management

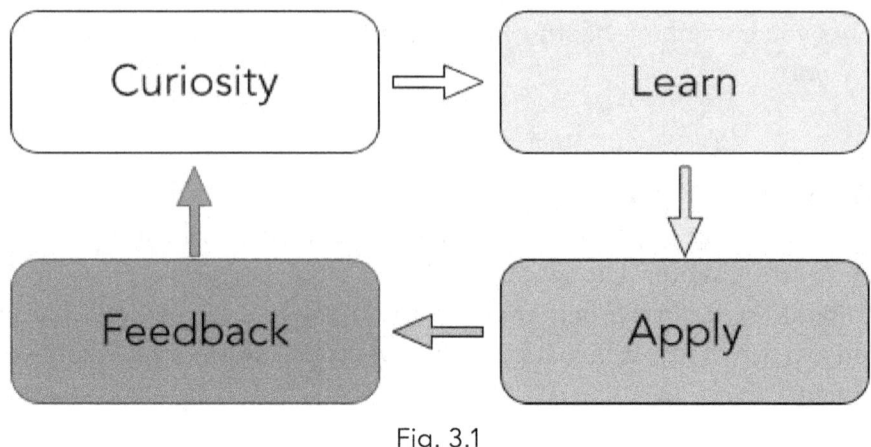

Fig. 3.1

The way many of us learned at school was not very effective because we were tested on subjects that we didn't find interesting. We were made to feel that failure was a bad thing, when the truth of the matter is that failure is inevitable and a key part of any progress.

In my school, it was compulsory to learn the language Afrikaans, and if we failed Afrikaans, we would fail the whole year. I had no great desire to learn Afrikaans, but I was forced to. Fortunately, I'm quite good at learning languages, so it wasn't a problem for me, but for others it was.

I remember a group of guys at school who used to ride motorbikes. They never really liked school and were much more interested in motorbikes. Their school grades were not very good, and they were constantly getting into trouble. The teachers wanted to make examples of them, so they made them out to be failures. This always amazed me because these same guys could strip down any motorbike and put it back together without any help. How could it be, then, that they were failures? Nobody else in school could do that. Unfortunately for them, the thing they were passionate about and quite skilled at was not something we were tested on, so that didn't count.

It is no coincidence that most people excel in subjects that they find interesting—or, at least, they had a teacher who inspired their curiosity in that subject. For me, my love of people, my curiosity for innovation, and the contribution of my role models inspired me to want to learn.

We are extremely fortunate to live in an age when there is so much great information and so many resources freely available to us, all in various media options, including the following:

* Books
* Online resources, such as videos and blogs
* DVD courses
* Workshops
* Seminars

As I am a visually creative person, I like videos, workshops, and seminars, the latter being my favorite because of interaction with other like-minded people.

Having a support group of like-minded individuals with whom you can discuss topics and share experiences is invaluable as you start to plot your own course of development and awareness. Remember, your current peer group may not share your enthusiasm for the subject you want to learn, so you will want to find like-minded people to support you.

Don't be afraid to seek out others for help and support, and above all, remember to keep it fun and enjoyable, and the results you achieve will be amazing.

Revise, Repeat, Remember

Learning information is one thing, but remembering it is not always easy. Have you ever had a situation where somebody asks you a question, and you are sure you know the answer, but you just can't remember? You get frustrated because you know the answer is in your head somewhere, but you just can't recall it. Then immediately after someone else says it, you remember. Or maybe you're telling a story, and you can't remember one of the details, so you finish the story without the missing information. Then an hour or so later, while you are doing something completely different, you remember what it was you wanted to say.

This happens to all of us. It's not that what we forget has gone from our memory; it's just that we struggle to recall it. Part of the problem comes from the state we were in when we first learned the information. If we were stressed or struggling to understand what we were trying to learn, we tend to store it haphazardly, making the information difficult to recall later.

Don't worry if this happens to you, because you can do something about it. Many different tools and techniques can help you remember.

Personally, I am a big fan of mind maps. As a visual person, I find mind maps are a great way for me to get information out of my head and onto paper. Once they are on paper this way, it is easy for me to visualize the big picture. I can also organize the detailed bits of information effortlessly because they can be moved around between sections and insert new items of information with ease as they come to me.

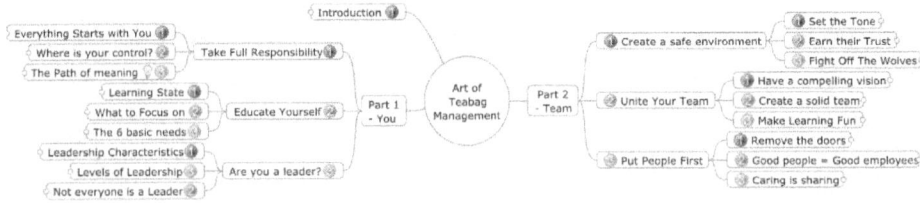

Fig. 3.2

If I am at a seminar or workshop and don't have direct access to my computer, I use highlighters and pencils to make notes on the handouts. Then as soon as I can, I put those notes into a mind map. Once I have the information captured in my mind maps, I revise the information three times in the following time frames:

* Twenty-four hours
* Seven days
* Thirty days

This first revision is key, as it allows me to see if the information still makes sense while it is fresh in my mind. Once I know it all makes sense, the seven-day and thirty-day revisions help make the information stick. This process works really well for me and helps me remember many of the key concepts I've learned, and it works irrespective of whether you choose to use mind maps.

Another great way to learn information is by repetition. Repeating the things you have learned over and over helps them take root in your memory. As a busy person, I get as much of the information as possible that I am learning downloaded in audio or video formats so that I can put it onto mobile devices like my smartphone.

Having the information stored on a mobile device makes it very easy for me to access it. I can then listen to the information while I'm driving, doing exercise, taking a walk, or sitting on a flight. I'm not necessarily always paying attention to the information consciously, but the information is being captured in my subconscious mind. This strategy takes very little effort or time, and I am still able to carry on doing other things that need to be done.

The Art of Tea Bag Management

I first started to use this technique when I was in high school, learning history. Because I am a creative and logical person, it is safe to say that history wasn't the most exciting subject for me. It involved writing long essays and remembering many key facts. I found storing and accessing the large amounts of information quite a challenge.

To overcome this challenge, I decided that whenever I had anything dense to study, I would simply read my notes aloud and record them onto my Walkman. Rather than having to read over my notes, I would just lie down, put my Walkman on, and listen. I would even go to sleep wearing my Walkman and just let the information continue while I slept.

At the time, I didn't have any scientific information to prove this approach worked; I just felt intuitively that it would, so I tried it. When I started to get positive results, I began to use it for all my subjects.

Section Summary

In this section of the book, I discussed things you can do to create a successful learning state. I spoke about the importance of curiosity as a key ingredient in learning and the benefits of making learning a fun experience. I also shared some tools and techniques to save you time and make learning easier.

A willingness to learn is a key characteristic of all great leaders, and the fact that you have bought this book shows you have already made a commitment to learning new skills. Some leaders may be born great, but everything they do can also be learned by you. In the next section, I focus on three key areas of development that every leader should know, and they are the fundamental skills required to master the art of tea bag management.

What to Focus On

I am often asked, "What is the one key skill all great leaders have in common?" The answer is, there isn't just one magic thing. I believe being a leader is not about having skills; it's about characteristics. And one of those characteristics is a desire to learn.

Many different situations require different skills. To lead people into battle would take a completely different set of skills than those required to teach a classroom full of children. A great leader recognizes which skills benefit a specific situation and then either learns the skills or builds a team of people who already have the required skills.

In this section of the book, I look at three fundamental skills that you need in order to implement the art of tea bag management.

1. Emotional Intelligence

When I left school, I was led to believe that IQ was the defining indicator of whether a person would be a success or a failure. As I was not very engaged at school, my teachers often used fear to try to engage me. To them, I showed all the signs of a child who was struggling to cope, but my exam results would always say something different—I did much better than they expected.

I left school with low self-esteem, believing I was an average person with no real prospect of being successful. I never did an IQ test at school because I was always afraid of what the result might be. I just blindly listened to my teachers, believing what they said to be true. In 2005, when I started to regain my power through learning on the Internet, I also started to regain my self-esteem. For the first time in my life, I had the courage to take an IQ test, and the results blew my mind. For years, I had listened to what other people had said without thinking to find out

The Art of Tea Bag Management

for myself. Now, seventeen years after leaving school, I discovered I had an IQ of 137. I was so shocked I decided to take it again, and this time it came back as 141.

The truth of the matter is that IQ is just a number. It made no difference in my life. What it did do, though, is make me realize things could have been very different if I had grown up in a more nurturing school environment. It also introduced me to another concept known as EQ: emotional quotient or emotional intelligence, which in my opinion is far more valuable and, more importantly, can be improved through education.

In a nutshell, emotional intelligence is a person's ability to understand, perceive, control, and evaluate emotions. As I mentioned in the previous paragraph, everything starts with you, so the more awareness you have over your emotions, the more control you have over your life. For me, this is the most important skill I could ever have, because everything else is affected by my emotional intelligence.

You can learn emotional intelligence, and there are many different ways to do so. Sometimes, tough experiences we go through in life actually help us develop emotional intelligence. For me, growing up with three older brothers played a big part in the development of my emotional intelligence. We tended to be quite competitive, so although we all got along really well, there was a lot of teasing and bullying going on. As the youngest brother, I got the lion's share of it, so I had to find ways to deal with the discomfort. I finally realized they wanted me to react when they teased me; they got what they wanted when I reacted, so they would do it repeatedly. When I saw this pattern, I taught myself not to react to their teasing, and eventually, because they were not getting the reaction they wanted, they stopped teasing me.

This taught me that although I couldn't stop *them* from doing what they wanted to do, I could control how *I* responded, and it was how I

responded that affected what they would do next. Emotional intelligence is the ability to recognize your emotions in any given situation and then choose a response that results in a positive outcome, regardless of how difficult it will be or how long it will take.

Emotional intelligence is also about understanding who you are and what beliefs you may have that cause you to react the way you do. Self-development is your key to unlocking your emotional-intelligence potential, and there are thousands of great self-development resources available, whether you undertake the journey alone or with the help of a professional coach. It is up to you to decide which way you want to go, but if I were to suggest a starting point, I would suggest going to a Tony Robbins event. I have spent the last nine years learning new self-development skills in a number of different areas, and in every one of those areas Tony Robbins has played a part in my learning, either directly or indirectly, by influencing and empowering those who have mentored me.

Mastering emotional intelligence is without a doubt the number one area everyone should learn. Regardless of whether you want to be a leader, having mastery of emotional intelligence will affect every single area of your life in a positive way.

2. Social Intelligence

While emotional intelligence is unquestionably the number one skill to learn, we have to be aware that we live in multicultural societies and interact with other people on a daily basis. As emotional intelligence focuses on how we react and respond to things, social intelligence is the ability to interact and negotiate with other people and the environment.

As a leader, social intelligence lies just below emotional intelligence on the scale of critical skills you need. I have met many brilliant people who have so much to give the world, but they have sometimes lacked the social intelligence that would allow them to communicate effectively with people around them. This lack of social intelligence makes it difficult to build rapport with others and can result in their becoming reclusive. When this starts to happen, they become frustrated and resentful; they begin to see the world as a bad place.

The great leaders of our time all have excellent social intelligence, which allows them to influence those around them. As with emotional intelligence, social intelligence is a skill that can be learned.

Depending on where you are on your journey of self-discovery, what I'm about to say may or may not seem quite deep, but bear with me because it will all make sense in the end.

Most people believe in dualism, which is a state in which we as individuals are separate from other people and the world around us. The belief is that when people go out into the world, they are individuals, with no connection to the things around them, and what they do has no effect on the people or the world around them. When people have this kind of mind-set, they are naturally more concerned about themselves than others. For a long time now, science and quantum physics have proven that this is actually not the case and that we are in fact all connected at the quantum level.

Without going into too much detail, science has proven we are connected to everything and everyone at the same time and that the actions we take affect everything and everyone in some way. Obviously, it's impossible for us to understand all the implications of this scientific, evidence-based theory, but accepting this as a concept will allow you to see the world in a different way from the average person.

Psychologists have also discovered that when humans are in groups, there is a phenomenon they call the social brain. The social-brain hypothesis suggests that human brains actually connect together in a group environment in a way similar to that found in large groups of animals. It is also known as the "morphogenetic field" and is a concept about resonance, which is spoken of in great depth by biologist and author Rupert Sheldrake.

Let's take, for example, a flock of birds. Flocks of birds have been recorded with as many as one billion birds in a single flock. There is no single leader in the flock, yet all the birds know exactly when to take off, when to turn, and when to land. This, too, comes down to the fact that the birds are in resonance with one another. They are connected to a social brain.

Understanding social intelligence and concepts like the social brain is key to being able to understand and lead a team of people. In a work environment, most managers lock themselves away in an office, detached from the people within their department. This restricts their ability to connect to their team and can result in a lack of influence and trust.

Social intelligence is an area in which I currently have a lot of interest, because human interaction is such an important value to me. I find

The Art of Tea Bag Management

it fascinating how we are all connected and how by helping the lives of others, we are, at the same time, improving our own world. I live by the ethos of Gandhi: "If we could change ourselves, the tendencies in the world would also change. As a man changes his own nature, so does the attitude of the world change toward him."

3. Human-Needs Psychology

Now that I have introduced the concepts of emotional and social intelligence, I want to spend a little bit of time looking at human-needs psychology and, in particular, the six basic human needs.

Human-needs psychology is a branch of psychology that looks at the individual in order to understand why we do the things we do. It is based primarily on the work of Milton Erickson, an American psychiatrist best known for his work with families, more recently made popular by the work of Cloé Madanes and Tony Robbins.

The underlying principle is that everything you have in your life now and everything you will have in the future comes down to the choices you make. You should notice a common theme throughout this book about taking responsibility for everything that happens in your life. It's understanding the different factors that make us do the things we do that is key to helping us make the necessary changes to move forward.

Humans possess six basic needs, which influence the choices we make. And they are the following:

* Certainty: our need to feel safe and secure
* Uncertainty: our need for variety, adventure, and surprise
* Connection or love: our need to feel loved and connected to others; we are social beings.
* Significance: our need for attention, to feel special
* Growth: our need to become better people
* Contribution: our need to contribute to others

These six human needs flow through all the areas of our lives including physical, financial, emotional, and spiritual. While we all share all six of these basic human needs, they are prioritized differently by each individual.

The Art of Tea Bag Management

Certainty
Individuals who place a high priority on certainty tend to be fearful of the world. Because they have a strong need for things to be a certain way, they can be quite controlling. Unfortunately, in life, the only thing we can ever be certain of is change. Having a strong desire for certainty in an ever-changing world can be extremely stressful.

Uncertainty
Individuals who prioritize uncertainty are much better at handling change. They love excitement and surprises, so they seek out activities and people who fulfill that need. They need to be careful not to change things just for the sake of changing them because, although change is inevitable, some things are best left alone.

Connection (Love)
The level of connection individuals need has a big effect on their ability to work alone. Individuals who place a high priority on connection tend to be quite needy, and in being needy, they actually make it more difficult for others to connect with them. Excessively independent people, on the other hand, can have difficulty connecting with people because they don't have a need for the connection. The sweet spot is in the middle, where you want connection, but you don't need it.

Significance
Significance can be the most destructive of the needs if it is given the highest priority. Under normal circumstances, significance is the need to feel wanted and important without wanting to be the center of attention. It is the need to feel that we are heard and that our contributions are valuable.

The dark side of significance is when the need is so great that the individual is willing to go to any lengths to feel significant. No expense is spared in the person's quest to fulfill his or her need for significance, be that in material goods or people. Such a person would do whatever he or she needed to feel significant.

Growth
Growth has been the theme throughout this chapter. As I mentioned previously, we all have a need to grow. So important is the need to grow that some people believe that when we stop growing, we start dying. When we stop using the muscles in our body, they become weak, and this concept also applies to our brains. Learning and growing are part of who we are; it is just that many of us went through a school system that didn't suit how we naturally learn, and it has turned us off from learning.

Contribution
Contribution is the need to be of service to others and goes beyond our own selfish needs. Unfortunately, contribution normally gets the lowest priority of all the human needs, but, together with growth, it makes up the most important needs within society. These two needs focus more on our abilities to improve the world as a whole. The first four needs focus more on the individual than the community and support the dualistic view of the world in that we are not connected.

Contribution and growth align with the view that we are all connected. As people become more aware of themselves and how they connect with others, the more enlightened they become. As they become more enlightened, they place greater priority on the needs of contribution and growth, for they realize the wisdom in the words of Aristotle when he said, "The whole is greater than the sum of its parts."

The Art of Tea Bag Management

My wish is that in some way, this chapter has made you curious enough to want to educate yourself in the personal skills like emotional and social intelligence. We can't truly consider ourselves leaders without first learning who we are and what makes us do the things we do. We don't necessarily have to do everything perfectly; we just need to know enough to know that we don't know everything and to be open to the fact that we may get things wrong from time to time. And that's OK.

In this chapter, I discussed how to create the most beneficial learning state: by being curious and by making learning fun. I also looked at the two key areas for you to focus on (emotional and social intelligence) and the concept of the six basic human needs to further develop your leadership skills.

In the next chapter, I look at some of the key characteristics of leaders that many of the great leaders of our time had in common.

Are You a Leader?

When I was a young boy, I believed that there was a group of elite people—leaders—who solved the problems of the world: a group of selfless, loving, and highly educated people who wanted the world to be a better place. I believed they looked at problems and things that needed improving and came up with solutions: solutions for the common good of all humankind.

Today, I still believe that these people exist. I still believe that there are people out there who are trying to make this world better for all of us, but they aren't the people I thought they were. Today I believe that we are those people, that we are the leaders, and that each and every one of us has far more potential than we could ever imagine. We just need someone to believe in us, to encourage us, and to help us become the best we can be. But most importantly, we have to believe in ourselves.

Not everyone is going to be an "ideas" person, and not everyone is going to want to "save the world," and that's OK, because leaders come in many different guises. True leaders believe that there is good in everyone, and they selflessly do everything in their power to create environments in which those around them can become leaders.

In this chapter, I look at some of the characteristics all great leaders share. I look at the differences between leaders and managers, and I explain how many companies are failing their people.

Leadership Characteristics

Since that day in March 2005 when I stumbled into the world of self-development, I have been introduced to a whole host of new role models I had no previous knowledge of. Finding these role models made me curious about leadership and what makes a good leader.

For me, having grown up in the extremely conservative apartheid South Africa and working in the high-stakes oil, gas, and petrochemical industries, most of the "leaders" I was exposed to tended to be quite forceful. In that, I mean their leadership style was quite hierarchical, leaving little room for debate or discussion. People were simply expected to do what they were told without question.

I've pondered the origins of this leadership style and believe that they can be traced back to the Second World War. During the war, leaders would have to make some tough decisions, like sending people who may never return out to fight. When making these kinds of decisions, one would need to be quite forceful, and that's understandable.

When the war ended, many of the high-ranking military people were then recruited as managers in the postwar economic boom, also known as the golden age of capitalism. This coincided with the baby boom and saw a new labor force entering the workplace under this hierarchical management style. For the baby boomers emerging into adulthood, this would have been the only management style they had ever have been exposed to, so it would be natural for them to adopt the same style when they became managers themselves.

Today, the world is a very different place compared to what it was back then, and the hierarchical management style is no longer suitable. The managers of the future will place more value on their people and on creating work environments that encourage creativity and innovation.

In this next section, I look at some of the characteristics of today's leaders with a view to understand what it is that makes them the great leaders they are.

Leadership Characteristics

I am often asked, "What makes a great leader?" It's a difficult question to answer because when I look at the people who inspire me—people like Nelson Mandela, Tony Robbins, Elon Musk, and Richard Branson—they are all very different people and have very different styles, yet they are all driven by a desire to make the world a better place.

To me, leaders are those who are willing to put themselves out in front, to put their head "above the parapet." They're willing to go against the crowd for the things they believe in, understanding that others do not always have the same capacity as their extraordinary vision. For them, their vision is so vivid that they can see the future as if it had already happened, and they use that vision to navigate toward their goals, never letting the opinions or doubts of others get in their way.

Leaders step up when things need changing. They don't just turn a blind eye when they see something is wrong, and they are willing to take on the anger of the crowd to try to put it right. They know that if they are not willing to stand up for what's right, then they can't expect anyone else to. Now that doesn't mean you have to try to resolve every problem that comes your way, but if it is a problem that affects you on an ongoing basis, then you are just as competent as anyone else to fix it.

The Art of Tea Bag Management

For some reason, the majority of people have come to believe it's just not their responsibility to solve issues unless the issue belongs solely to them. They'd much rather moan and complain about the problems than actually get up and do something about them, as if it were somebody else's responsibility to fix it for the collective. Leaders do the right thing even when nobody is looking.

Great leaders are open with people, and they tell others when they cannot share something. This may sound contradictory, but I know firsthand what it's like to have information that—for sensitivity reasons—cannot be passed on. In my experience, people don't mind if you hold back information as long as you tell them so, rather than pretending that you don't have the information in the first place. Not only do they respect you for telling them the truth, but it also makes them trust you more.

I pride myself on being open and honest with the people with whom I work. In fact, I find it a great honor and privilege to serve them and help them grow and become better people. At all times, I have their best interests at heart, and as they get to know me, they realize that really is the case. By building up this great rapport with them, I instill their trust in me—a trust I will not violate because their well-being really is my number one priority.

Another common trait I see in great leaders is humility. They don't expect people to do things they wouldn't do themselves. They never ask people to do jobs for them if they wouldn't be prepared to do themselves. And if they were required to do it, they would, without question.

In the previous chapter, I discussed education and how great leaders have a desire for knowledge—knowledge they can use for the greater good of the whole team and pass on to individuals if required. Leaders are the teachers and the role models for the next generation, and they realize a major part of being a leader is creating more leaders. They know far more can be accomplished by having many leaders as opposed to just one.

Leaders inspire people by sharing visions of the future. They keep people focused on moving forward rather than giving up and staying where they are. They know the importance of progress, no matter how small, and are always willing to help people move forward.

In times of crisis, great leaders stay calm. They know in times of uncertainty when people are scared or confused that people will look to them for guidance, and if they are calm and assured, then people will feed off their assuredness and be calm, too.

Richard Branson best describes one of the greatest traits of a leader in a recent article. In it, Branson asked someone who worked closely with Nelson Mandela what it was that made Nelson Mandela such a great leader. One of the things Mandela's associate said was, "His actions come from the perspective of what's right for someone in the village. He has no personal agenda." This mentality epitomizes what makes a leader great: the desire to always want to do what's right for the whole and not just for a part of the whole.

In the previous chapter, I spoke about dualism and about how most people live in a reality where they feel separate from the things around them. It is obvious from the above comments that Nelson Mandela does not share such a belief. He understands at a very deep level that we are all connected.

Of course, great leaders share many other traits, but the ones I have covered in this section are the most significant. You see, it is not what we do that makes us great, it's who we are and what we stand for. It's who we are that affects the choices we make and the actions we take, not the other way around.

Levels of Leadership

For many people, the idea of becoming a great leader, like those mentioned previously, seems so far away from where they are now that it seems impossible. While I agree it can take a long time to reach the lofty heights of those great leaders, the first step is simply to make a decision, a decision that you no longer want to be a bystander in your life and that you know intuitively at a deep level that you are a part of something bigger than yourself.

To explain this to people in my workshops, I use the analogy of a giant redwood tree. Like all trees, the giant redwood starts out as a seed. The seed is placed in fertile ground, where it starts to grow its roots. With its roots spreading out in the nurturing soil, the seed receives all the important nutrients it needs in order to grow. The more developed the root structure, the more nutrients the seed is able to absorb from the nurturing soil, and so the more likely it is that it will grow to be a giant redwood tree. You see, even as a seed, it is still a giant redwood tree. It just hasn't reached its full potential yet.

As with all things in life, it takes a little time and effort, but once you have decided on the outcome, it is just a matter of seeing it through to the end. As you set off on your path to becoming a leader, you will develop your communication skills on four significant levels:

1. Yourself
2. One-on-one
3. Teams or groups
4. Communities, cultures, or countries

T E **A** C U P

As I've mentioned throughout this book, everything starts with you, and the development path to become a leader is no different. You start by educating yourself in leadership skills like self-motivation, discipline, contribution, and emotional intelligence, as mentioned in the previous chapter.

Self-talk is extremely important, and the language we use to ourselves can be very powerful. To make the changes I mention in this book will require a lot of will power. Some days you will want to quit and just go back to your comfort zone. Talking to yourself in a positive and constructive way and using empowering language will help to drive you forward. Negative self-talk can be very destructive, so you would do well to be aware of your communications with yourself.

As you develop these skills, you start to gain more control of yourself, which will increase your self-confidence and belief. This new confidence will allow you to start exploring the world and help you stretch your comfort zone by putting you in new situations. By stepping outside of your comfort zone, you meet new people, experience new things, and see new ways of doing things. In fact, all learning and growth starts outside the comfort zone.

Once you have started working on yourself, you will notice that people are drawn to you. They notice a change in you and want to know what you did. At this point, you enter the second level of leadership because you are now in a position where you can make a positive impact on another person.

This can be something as small as taking the time just to listen to what that person has to say without any need to say anything to them. If in that moment you give them your full attention and empathy, you could make a massive impact on their life because so few people ever have an opportunity to say how they feel, not knowing that someone is actively listening. All too often, when people are telling us their problems, we feel we have to respond, so instead of listening, we are thinking about what we are going to say next.

> **WISE MEN SPEAK BECAUSE THEY HAVE SOMETHING TO SAY; FOOLS BECAUSE THEY HAVE TO SAY SOMETHING**
>
> - Plato

Once you have started to influence people on a one-to-one basis, you will find that people begin to see you as the voice of reason. When this happens, you will have moved into the third level of leadership, in that you are now able to influence groups of people.

Reaching this level is no easy feat, as most people never even reach self-mastery. When looking at the communication levels, to reach this third level is probably the most significant because to reach this point you will have extremely high emotional intelligence and—at minimum—a very good grasp of social intelligence.

Having such ability in these core skills will hold you in good stead when moving toward the next and final leadership level, the level where you are influencing communities, cultures, or countries.

The major ingredients in moving from the third to the fourth level are exposure and courage. There are many ways to gain exposure like joining social, political, or community groups in whatever area that you want to get involved in. The more exposure you gain, the more you will be able to communicate your ideas to the world. Here, again, your emotional and social intelligence will come to the fore.

The downside to increased exposure is that it tends to come with increased criticism—and this is where courage comes in. We all have two primal fears. The first is that "we won't be loved," and the second is that "we are not good enough." Both of these fears will come to the fore as you start to show yourself to the world and share your ideas. Your courage will help you keep moving forward in the face of fear.

As people, we are all driven by different needs, so no two paths of leaders will ever be exactly the same. Some may want to progress all the way to the top level of leadership, while others are happy with getting to the first level. For me, the first level is by far the most important of the four levels because in reaching that first level, a leader is born. Regardless of the level you go on to achieve, it is the first phase that creates the leader.

One important distinction I must make is that you cannot force your way through the levels. If you have to force your way through any level, you are not a leader; you are more of a dictator. And you are not leading; you are controlling, the dangers of which I discussed in the second chapter of this book.

Not Everyone Is a Leader

During my career, I have worked on three different continents for over twenty different clients, including oil companies, EPC contractors, and oil and gas service companies. Within those organizations, I have worked with men and women from all over the world, including America, Angola, Brazil, Holland, Kazakhstan, Korea, Nigeria, Portugal, Russia, and South Africa, to name but a few. I have encountered numerous different management styles influenced by a multitude of different factors such as culture, gender, and age.

What I noticed was that the characteristics that defined both the good and bad managers were universal and crossed all borders. In that,

I mean they all shared similar leadership traits regardless of where they were from, their genders, or their ages. Understandably, some cultures had biases toward certain types of management styles, but never were they universal. This proved to me that leadership is based on character and nothing else.

When Promotions Fail

By now, you have probably noticed that this book focuses more on leadership than it does on management, which almost contradicts the title of the book. The reason I did that is that, for me, managers should be leaders. When I talk about bad managers, I don't mean they are bad people; what I'm saying is that they shouldn't be managers. Now that may be a harsh thing to say, but it's what I truly believe.

In my opinion, the commonly accepted idea about what a manager is, is wrong. And I don't blame the managers for the current situation. Somewhere along the line, we fell into a trap in which in order to reward someone for doing a good job or for their loyalty, we would increase their salary. In order to increase the salary and avoid a potential conflict with coworkers earning different salaries for doing the same job, companies decided to promote people.

While this solved the problem of justifying a higher salary, it often meant that people without any of the leadership skills mentioned in this book were now responsible for teams of people. Just because someone is good at their job doesn't necessarily mean they will be a good manager.

This occurrence is more commonly known as the "Peter Principle," from the 1969 book of the same name by Laurence J. Peter and Raymond Hull. The principle states that, "[m]embers of an organization where promotion is based on achievement, success and merit will eventually be promoted beyond their level of ability." The principle is the origin of the phrase: "employees tend to rise to their level of incompetence."

Although the Peter Principle has been around for over four decades, companies have done very little about it. For me, it can result in two significantly detrimental effects. The first is that once someone is promoted, it means they are now controlling a team, and if they are incompetent, the entire team is affected. Secondly, just because the person was good in his or her previous role does not necessarily mean they will be able to cope with the additional responsibility the new role brings. It can be a double-edged sword as you lose an extremely effective employee and gain an ineffective manager.

Not only does this affect the company, but it can also affect all the individuals involved by creating additional stress and resentment. This may sound far-fetched, but I have personally witnessed this on at least two occasions. On both occasions, the companies were desperate to fill positions left open by people leaving, but because they hadn't done anything about developing the people they already had on the team, they didn't have suitable candidates to take over when the manager moved on.

This created a situation where they were desperate to find someone to fill the role, and the most qualified person in the team was desperate to have the job, but he lacked the required leadership skills. Stuck between a rock and a hard place, the company eventually decided that he was the best option and promoted him to the management role.

The rest of the team members were extremely resentful, and some immediately started looking for new jobs. The new manager tried his best to get everyone onboard by trying to be overly friendly; his lack of interest in them before the promotion was now coming back to haunt him.

People aren't stupid, and they can tell when someone is being inauthentic—especially when they have worked with that person for a period of time beforehand. In fact, trying to be friendly just to win someone's trust is the worst thing to do because it does the exact opposite, causing *distrust* in the person instead.

The way to avoid this situation would have been to call a meeting with everyone affected by the decision and have a free and open discussion so that everyone was aware of the difficulties in replacing the previous manager. You would then give everyone an opportunity to share their thoughts and discuss possible solutions. Once all possible solutions have been discussed, you can look to make a decision with everybody's consent. If there is still no clear decision, then you could take a vote based on the best possible options.

There is no guarantee that everyone would be happy with the outcome, but because everybody's input was taken into consideration, and the decision was made as a team, people would be more prepared to accept the final decision.

Two Types of Respect

Often in management circles, I hear comments about the importance of respect or how their people don't respect them. The thing is, respect is not something you are "entitled" to as a manager. The ironic thing is that managers who aren't worried about getting respect tend to get it, but the ones who are often don't.

A few years ago, I read an article that stated there are two types of respect:

1. Respect from fear; and
2. Respect from admiration.

Respect from fear applies to those leaders who use fear and force to control people. They bark orders at people to get them to do what they want, without taking the time to sit them down and see if they understand what needs to be done.

I had the chance to witnesses this in detail recently. A colleague who was working with me at the time was the manager for the department located right next to mine. It actually worked out to be the ideal situation for me to test out my management style against the more traditional hierarchical management style of my colleague.

Whenever there was a problem, he would get irritated and frustrated. He would then get angry with his team and start shouting orders at them to fix whatever was wrong. Most of the time, his team members weren't clear on what needed to be done, but this didn't matter as long as they were doing something. They didn't feel like they could ask for clarity on what they needed to do. This made them inefficient because they weren't 100 percent sure of what they were doing. They were also afraid to make any mistakes for fear of being punished. Needless to say, the manager was rarely happy with the efforts of his team. This in turn meant he would have more heated conversations with his team. It was as if they were in a constant figure eight of negativity where nothing ever had a chance to heal.

Watching this from the outside was extremely revealing. It was so obvious what this pattern of frustration and irritation was doing to his team. The constant arguments and shouting meant he didn't have the support of his team, and this made him feel as if he had to do everything himself. In my opinion, if anything has to be forced out of someone, it is not worth having. I guess it's a bit like beating a confession out of a witness; the witness will say whatever you want him or her to say, which really makes the confession worthless.

The Art of Tea Bag Management

For me, respect is earned, not forced. The reason the leaders who get respect (even if they don't need it) get it is because they do things for others unconditionally. They serve others without the need for anything in return, and people admire that quality in them. On the back of the admiration comes respect, and while I am sure they are all extremely grateful and appreciative of the respect, it's not why they do what they do. They do it because their desire to contribute is of such high importance to them.

Do You Really Care?

In the past three paragraphs, I discussed a number of key components of leadership. I also discussed some of the characteristics of leaders. The truth is that we are all different, and we all see the world in different ways. The information and concepts I have shared in this book resonate with me because they reflect who I am as a person. You, though, may not be like me; you may not see the world the way I see it.

When I ask the question, "Do you really care?" I ask it from a place of sincerity and not to be facetious, because everyone has the right to do things the way they want to do them. If nothing I have said resonates with you or inspires you to want to lead with more empathy, then there is nothing wrong with that. Being a great leader is not easy; it's not a walk in the park, and it takes a lot of dedication and effort—and that's not for everybody—so I really do understand.

I am guessing, though, that if you are still reading this, you do want to become a better leader, and I honor you for stepping up. We face many problems in today's world, and it is up to us as individuals and as leaders to play our part in making the world a better place. It all starts with a commitment to yourself to be a better person and, ultimately, a better leader. As you start to work on the various areas of your life, you will start to see the results of your actions coming to fruition. This won't happen overnight, but if you keep doing a little bit to move forward, then you will experience the rewards.

I know when I first set out on my journey, I didn't always acknowledge what I had achieved, but whenever I met up with friends whom I hadn't seen for a while, they were amazed at how much I had changed. Sometimes we don't notice how far we have come because we are constantly observing ourselves, so it helps to get out and see friends because they will notice the difference.

Additionally, it is vitally important that you reward yourself for making progress. This will keep you motivated and give you mini-milestones to work toward.

Remember, it all starts with your decision to make a difference. In subsequent chapters of this book, I turn the focus toward the implementation of the art of tea bag management and show you step-by-step how to do it.

Part Two

Implementing the Art of Tea Bag Management

In part one of this book, I focused on the manager and looked at some of the core skills and characteristics that make a good manager. Part one focused on three areas, with each covered in a separate chapter:

- **T** — Take Responsibility
- **E** — Educate Yourself
- **A** — Are You a Leader?

In this part of the book, I look at the actual implementation and the key ingredients to successfully implement the art of tea bag management. It is important to note that while these principles can be implemented by anyone at any stage of their development, the core management skills discussed in part one play a significant role in being able to make this process a success.

I say this because much of what I will share with you in this part of the book is counterintuitive, and those around you may not understand what you are doing and may become critical. Like most things done properly, it takes time before you start seeing results, so you have to stay diligent while you are putting the pieces in place.

Using the mnemonic used throughout this book, we are now focusing on the:

As with part one, part two is divided into three main sections, with each section covered in a separate chapter. Below is a diagram detailing the three sections.

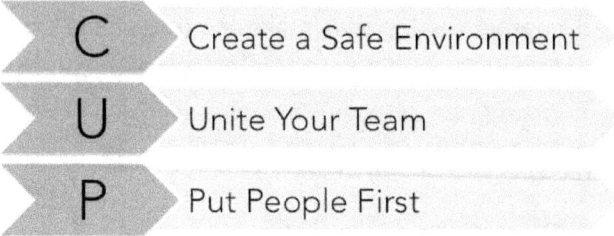

Create a Safe Environment

While each of the three sections covered in part two of this book is equally important, creating a safe environment is critical to making the whole thing work. This basic element allows everything else to work. Just as in the metaphor used throughout this book, the safe environment is symbolized by the teacup. Without it, you simply cannot make a cup of tea.

Set the Tone

This may sound obvious, but the first thing you need to do is review everything as it is now. You can do this by yourself, or sit down with everyone concerned and gather as much information as you can about everything that is going on in your team. Remember that, as discussed in part one of this book, as the leader, you will be taking complete responsibility for everything and everyone in your area of supervision, so it pays to know exactly what that looks like. Good or bad, it is in your best interest to get as much feedback as you can.

The Art of Tea Bag Management

Once you have had a chance to review all the feedback and take stock of everything that is going on, arrange to meet your team. By "team," I mean everyone who falls under your supervision—not just your management team or your key team members. Remember, you are building a culture here, so everyone should be involved.

It is during this first meeting that you start to set the tone for everything else to follow, so start as you mean to continue. Don't try to do it all in one go; you want to use this first meeting to set the tone for what's to come. Let everyone know that, from this point on, you will be taking full responsibility for everything that happens in your area of responsibility. You have been given the leadership role, so you will accept all the responsibility associated with that role. Tell your team that they no longer have to worry about what others outside of the department are saying. If somebody has an issue with a team member or with what that person is doing, then that person taking issue should speak to you, and you will address it. Your team members are not to be concerned with such matters.

Secondly, let them know there is no such thing as failure. I personally don't believe anyone does something with the intention of doing it wrong. If people make mistakes and do things "wrong," it is normally because they think either what they did was right, or they didn't know how to do it any other way. Regardless of the reason, it is your responsibility as the manager to teach them how to do it the way you want them to. Let them know that mistakes happen and that you will take full responsibility for any mistakes that happen.

Also let them know that your number one priority is your team. Their needs are your top priority, and you are always available for them when they have a problem, both professionally and personally. Managers manage, and it is your responsibility to ensure that you have sufficient time to manage.

A common problem I have seen repeatedly throughout my career is when people who are extremely good at their jobs are promoted to management positions as a reward for their contributions. Unfortunately, they receive no management training and simply continue to do what they do well, but with the title of manager. Being good at a job does not mean you will be good as a manager. The two require completely different skill sets. If you assume the role of a manager but continue to work with the same mentality as you did before, you will very quickly become stuck in a situation where you take on so much work that you will not have time to manage your team. As a manager, you will be assessed on the performance of the whole team, not just on your contribution. Stepping back from the day-to-day tasks and delegating them to your team to handle while you focus on managing the team would better serve you.

> ## THE WHOLE IS GREATER THAN THE SUM OF ITS PARTS
> - Aristotle

Create an environment where your team members always feel able to come and talk to you. I say that not just from the point of being open and willing but also by letting them see you are available. If your desk is covered in papers and you're always busy, they will be reluctant to come and see you when they need help because they will not want to disturb you. This is natural and something many of us learned as a child. Most of us have had experiences of wanting the attention of our parents, but because they were busy doing something, they told us to go away and play or watch TV.

Your focus as manager should be on the major issues, the risky ones that carry the most responsibility. Day-to-day issues are best done by your team, giving you the time and headspace you need to handle any unforeseen issues that might arise. You want to be able to handle them in a calm and composed manner.

If you're already operating at full speed and something unforeseen arises, it will push you over the edge and likely make you extremely stressed and agitated. You want to avoid this at all costs because this will manifest in the team in one way or another. Like dropping a stone into a pond, it will send ripples through the water. This can make your team feel uneasy about coming to see you with their problems or when seeking advice.

Remember, in this initial meeting, you are simply setting the tone for what's to come. You don't have to cover everything at this point. If you are already responsible for a team and you want to make changes, it will help to let them know why you're doing what you're doing because if you don't, they may not trust your intentions.

Earn Their Trust

Once you have set the tone for what's to come, you need to start earning their trust. I say "earning" because some managers believe trust should be given to them simply because they are the boss, as if it is an entitlement. You may have noticed that throughout this book I avoid using the word *employee*. I have done this because we are all people; we are not "employees." Just because we have jobs does not mean we are no longer people. All too often, we forget that business is still about people dealing with people and that, just as in normal life where we need to first earn someone's trust, the same is true in the work environment.

I believe we should always strive to earn people's trust, and this shouldn't be a difficult thing to do. As a leader, trust is the key requirement because it allows your team members to see you as an authority. In

TEA **C** UP

Robert Cialdini's book *Influence: The Psychology of Persuasion*, he suggests there are six key principles of influence, one of which is authority. He states that people will tend to obey authority figures even when asked to perform objectionable acts. So having your team see you as an authority will be extremely beneficial to your cause.

The easiest way to earn people's trust is to trust them first. So often in today's society we tend to distrust people, so if you can demonstrate that you trust them, then they will very likely return the favor.

Another thing you can do is let them know that you, too, are human and that you make mistakes just like anybody else. Let them know you have made mistakes and that you are probably going to make more in the future. People in general tend to be very wary of anything that seems to be too good to be true, so being open, honest, and OK with showing your vulnerability will make it easier for them to trust you.

> **MAN IS LEAST HIMSELF WHEN HE TALKS IN HIS OWN PERSON. GIVE HIM A MASK AND HE WILL TELL YOU THE TRUTH.**
> - Oscar Wilde

In one of my management roles, I inherited a team of people who had been severely neglected for a number of years. They were extremely distrustful of the management team and also—understandably—afraid of what my plans might be for the future. Because I was new to the company, they had no idea what to expect, so they were very closed when I first arrived. When I held my first meeting with them to set the tone for what was to come, it was very evident that there was a lack of trust—more than I had ever experienced before.

The Art of Tea Bag Management

It was clear they had stuff they wanted to say, but because of the lack of trust, I could see they were afraid to open up to me. To overcome this, I did something quite simple. I asked them to e-mail me with any problems they wanted raised but were afraid to say out in the open. I knew, however, that they might still be hesitant to e-mail me for fear of retribution, so I did something I'd never done before. I created an e-mail account in Google and gave everyone the access details so they could log into the e-mail account and send anonymous e-mails to me with the problems they wanted to raise. This did two very powerful things: first, it gave them a way to talk about things they were not comfortable saying openly, and second, it showed them that I was someone they could trust, someone who really did want to make things better.

It was no surprise, however, that no one actually used the e-mail address. The mere act of offering it made them trust me so much that they never felt they had to use it.

As I mentioned earlier, I don't think trust should be a difficult thing to achieve, but that's because I am an extremely trusting person, and others may not share the same trait. Again, this goes back to our conditioning and our life experiences, so whatever your current views are about trust is OK. It is a skill that can be learned.

Open and honest communication is important for building trust. Let people know where you are and what you're thinking, and let them know how you arrived at the decisions you made. Of course, there will be times when you can't tell them everything, but tell them that, and explain to them why.

I have no problem opening up to people because I have a fundamental belief that I never do anything to intentionally hurt someone else. Of course, there may be times when things I do make people feel hurt, but that is never my intention. We cannot control how people react to the things we do because it's up to them to place meaning on the things they see or experience. But because I know intrinsically that I am not doing something with the intention of hurting them, I am able to look people in the eye and explain why I did what I did.

Earlier in this book, I spoke about the principle of dualism. It is an idea that we are all individual beings and are not connected. I, however, believe in "singularity," which is a view that we are all connected and that everything that happens in the world around me affects me. If I were to upset somebody or cause them harm, I would inadvertently be harming or upsetting myself. No part of me wants to "get one over" on someone else because we would both be losing something.

I don't expect everyone to share my views, but I think it is important for you to know where I'm coming from when I share some of my concepts. I'm happy to discuss them, and I understand that not everybody will share my views, but being open and honest about them allows me to build trust with people because they know I am not holding back. Doing similarly with your team will significantly increase how much they trust you.

At the end of the day, when we strip everything away, business is about people, and people like people whom they can trust. I love all people. I think everyone is doing the best they can with the knowledge and the resources they have available to them.

One of my prime foci, as a manager, is not to create great employees; it is to create great people. I believe people become great employees as a by-product of being great people, not the other way around. I strive to inspire people to make their lives the best they can, to make them believe

The Art of Tea Bag Management

they are capable of doing so much more than they are when I first meet them. It is my goal to leave every person I have the privilege to work with in a better position than they were in when I arrived. And I'm extremely proud to say I have achieved my goal nearly every time.

I go above and beyond what is expected of me to develop the people I work with because I truly get the value of a strong team over a group of strong individuals. By building their trust in me, I'm also getting them to trust in one another. I look at each person individually, but I am always conscious of the big picture.

Each member of the team will probably be at a different level with regard to development, so a "one-size-fits-all" approach can have mixed results. As a way to explain my approach to development, I use an analogy of a leaky jug.

Imagine a one-liter, clear plastic jug with a number of holes spread randomly around the jug. If I were to tell you to fill the jug with water, you would start to fill the jug until you hit the first hole, and the water would start to leak out of the jug. At this point, you might be inclined to stop filling the jug and leave it with enough water to take you up to the first hole. You'd be quite happy to use the jug but only up to the point before the hole so that you don't have any water leaking out. That is obviously a very sensible thing to do, and not many people would question your reasoning. But the jug could potentially be used to carry more water if the leaks were not there at all.

Because I want people to reach their full potential, I would fill the jug until I hit the first hole. Then I would see how I could fix the hole. Once I had fixed the first hole, I would put more water in the jug until I got to the next hole, and I would continue the process until the jug had reached its full potential.

T E A C U P

While some people will see the leaks as a bad thing and write the jug off, I just see the leaks for what they are and fix them. With the people I am responsible for, I never shy away from giving them more and more responsibility because, until I know where their "leaks" are, I don't know what I need to do to help them repair their leaks.

I make it very clear that failure is not a bad thing and that making mistakes is actually a vital part of improvement. All the great leaders and great inventors of our time are very aware that failure is part of the process and that, in failure, there are lessons that help us move forward.

If people in your team make a mistake and you reprimand them, they will become fearful of making further mistakes, and this will severely affect their initiative. But if you were to explain to them that it is your responsibility to help them learn and that what they did was a natural part of development, then they would be more inclined to try again. As they learn that you *do* have their best interests at heart and that you are committed to helping them develop, their trust in you will increase, and their development will increase exponentially. It really is a win-win process for all concerned.

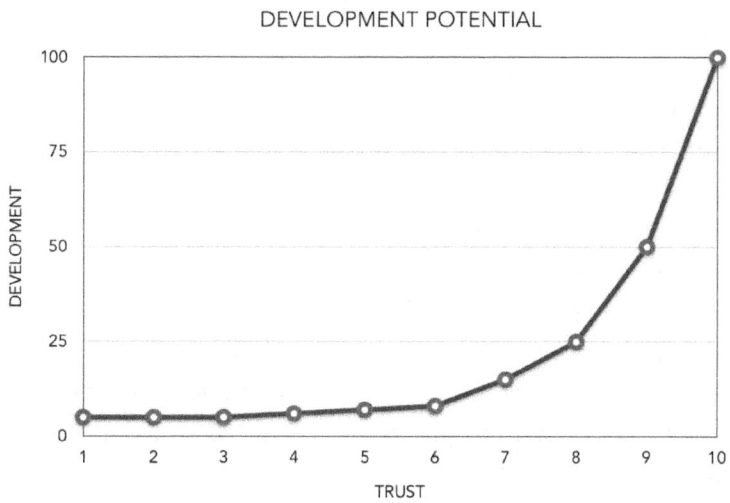

The Art of Tea Bag Management

One of the things that holds people back in their development is fear of making bad decisions. In school, we learned there were good decisions and bad decisions. If we made a bad decision, we normally ended up in trouble. No, I am not going to say that there are no bad decisions because it is the decisions we make that give us the results we get, both good and bad.

What I do think about decisions, though, is this: very few decisions are fatal, in the sense that there is no undoing what was done. As humans, we are going to make mistakes. We just have to take responsibility for the decisions we make and admit when we make a mistake. I believe there is far more danger in not making any decision than there is in making a bad decision.

As long as you know what the outcome is you are looking for, you can recover—no matter which decision you make. The truth of the matter is that once you've made a decision, you can never really compare it to the other choice that you had because, unless you've actually done something, you have no idea how it would've turned out. Most people tend to be overly optimistic about what would've happened had a different decision been made, especially when the decision made didn't turn out exactly as they had wanted. Imagine you and a friend are driving somewhere you had never been before. You know the area, but you don't know exactly which way to go. You pull up to a T-junction, and neither of you knows if you should go left or right. After several minutes of deliberating, you decide to go left, but your friend thought you should have gone right. You arrive at your destination a little late, and your friend is adamant that had you turned right, you would've arrived on time. While there is every chance that your friend may have been right, there is no way of knowing if turning right would have made any difference at all. Because you didn't go right, you have no way of knowing if there might have been construction or a car accident that would have made you arrive even later than you did. What is certain, though, is that by turning left or

right—making a decision—you got to your destination much quicker than if you had sat at the T-junction without having made a decision.

I tend to handle decisions like this. If I have a couple of choices and there is a very obvious "best" choice, I take it because all the information I have available suggests that it is a much better choice than any other option available. If, however, there is no obvious "best" choice, I pick any one of those available as long as it is obvious that is not a "bad" choice.

It's far too easy to get hung up on making the *right* choice and putting too much emphasis on the outcome. Whatever happens, there is probably a very good chance that you will be able to handle whatever happens, so don't get analysis paralysis.

A Decision Exercise

In the below image there are three pairs of cubes (A / B / C)

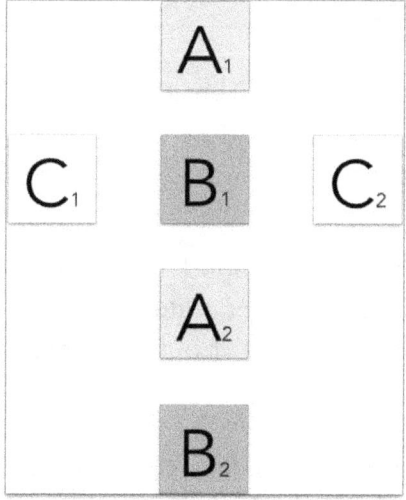

The Decision Exercise

69

The Art of Tea Bag Management

The rules of the exercise are as follows:

* You have sixty seconds to complete the exercise.
* You have to draw a line from:
    * A1 to A2,
    * B1 to B2, and
    * C1 to C2.
* Your lines are NOT allowed to:
    * go through any of the cubes,
    * run along the outside lines of the cubes,
    * go outside the boundary of the paper, or
    * touch or cross any other line.

You have sixty seconds to decide whether this can or can't be done, and your time starts **NOW.**

How did you do? If you managed to complete the exercise without breaking any of the rules, then congratulations, you are in the 2 percent of people who manage to figure it out and, more importantly, are not afraid to make a decision.

Ninety-eight percent of people will not have figured it out, and that is completely understandable given the way most of us have been conditioned. So much of society is about fitting in and being afraid to fail that we find it difficult to make decisions until we are confident we know that we are making the right choice.

In this exercise, the majority of people would not have drawn a single line because they couldn't see how it would work. Rather than try, they would have had analysis paralysis. The ironic thing is that there wasn't really any decision to make. The instructions actually stated exactly what to do.

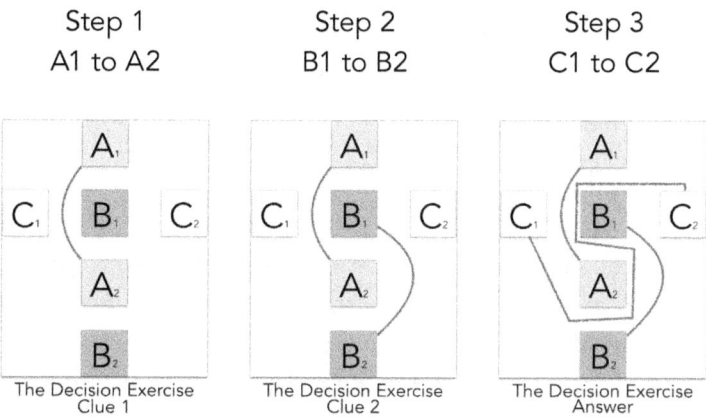

Step 1
A1 to A2

Step 2
B1 to B2

Step 3
C1 to C2

The Decision Exercise Clue 1

The Decision Exercise Clue 2

The Decision Exercise Answer

As with many of the other concepts I have discussed in this book, this approach to decision-making may not seem natural, but I assure you they can all be learned. They just take a little bit of practice and perseverance. The more you apply them, the better you will get.

Don't be afraid to let people know what you're doing, because they will probably be more supportive than you imagine, especially those in your team, because you're doing this for their benefit, too.

I also hope that once you have learned the skills mentioned in this book, you pass them on to the people in your team. It's best to share knowledge, not keep it a secret.

The Art of Tea Bag Management

Fighting Off the Wolves

Once you have set the tone within your team and they trust you enough to believe that what you want to do will work, you still have to be mindful, as people on the outside looking in may not know what you're doing. Things may have been done a certain way for a long time, and when you start to apply the things I teach in this book, people may not be supportive.

Because change can be disruptive, not everybody is open to it. In the third chapter, I spoke about the six basic human needs, one of which is certainty. People who have certainty as one of their primary needs will probably be afraid of what you're doing. No matter how good or bad the current situation is, their need for certainty will be so great that they will want to leave things as they are, irrespective of whether the outcome will be a benefit to them.

Chances are, they will first raise their concerns with you, but once they realize you are going to follow through on your plans, they may be inclined to try to influence the members of your team. If you have done a good job in setting the tone for the future and earning their trust, it is highly likely that your team will not be swayed by the outside influence.

Unfortunately, the antagonists won't stop from trying to disrupt your plans. The next thing they will probably try is to discredit you or your plans. At this point, it is important you make yourself the filter between any negativity happening outside and the positive environment you are creating inside. Take any criticism or negativity with a pinch of salt. If there are any real concerns or things that need to be improved, then put them on your list of things to do, but do them in line with what you are already doing. It is important you stick to your plan and not get overrun by other people's demands.

The beginning is always the hardest time as you try to juggle responsibility of the overall company needs and your plan to implement these new ideas. It can feel like you're fighting a battle on two fronts, but it is important you stay calm and resolute. Any sign of weakness during these early stages can have a detrimental effect on your plans.

A key part of getting you through these initial stages is being consistent with the message you are putting out, both internally and externally. Remember, people are still getting to know you, and you are building trust with your team, so they will want to know that you are following through on what you said and not just paying lip service. If they sense you are starting to react to the wishes of others, then you risk losing the confidence and support of your team.

In this chapter, we looked at the first major step in implementing the art of tea bag management: creating a safe environment. This starts by getting everyone together and setting the tone for what is to come. You then start to work on earning their trust by being available to them, helping them develop, and removing any fear or blame. Finally, we looked at keeping away the wolves, being resolute in your approach, and protecting your team from any potential negativity and hostility from outside.

These are the initial steps to help you get things moving, and in the next chapter, I look at building on the initial actions to create a strong and united team.

Unite Your Team

In the previous chapter, I looked at how to create a safe environment, symbolized by the cup in the metaphor. Now I turn our focus to the second part: the water. The water symbolizes the environment and the culture within the department, and, as in nature, water is the key to life and growth.

Many of the top-performing corporate companies have realized the importance of creating a more collaborative, harmonious culture and an enjoyable, nurturing working environment that makes their people happy and excited about going to work.

Companies like Google, Facebook, Zappos, and Apple have taken full advantage of this knowledge and instead of having hardworking, stressed employees, they have created armies of diehard loyal fans—people who love being part of the companies they work for and the vision those companies promote. For most of your customers, both internal and external, a large factor in determining how they feel about you and your team will come from their interactions with the individuals within it. If you create a loyal, vibrant team, they become your ambassadors and will have a significantly positive effect on your customers' experiences.

On the negative side, bad working environments have a detrimental effect on companies. They lower the morale of the people and thus create unhappy and stressful environments. In recent years, numerous studies have been carried out to evaluate the impact this has on businesses. Research carried out in the United States estimates that lost workdays caused by stress costs up to **$30 billion** a year while the annual lost-productivity costs were a staggering **$200 billion**.

The figures below show some of the results of employee surveys carried out in the United States:

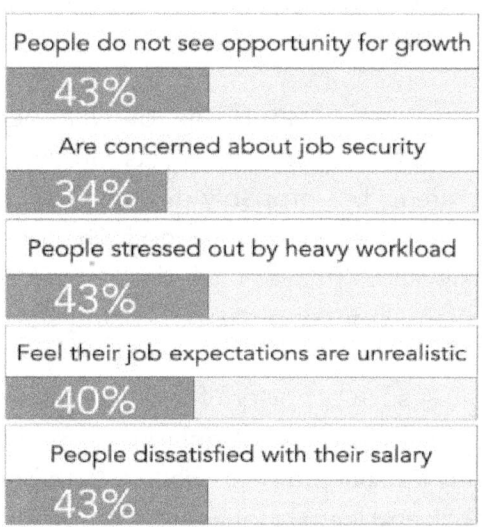

While the statistics may show a bleak picture, you can improve them quite dramatically by making changes to the culture and the work environment. In this chapter, I look at what you can do to make those changes.

Have a Compelling Vision

> **IT IS TRUE OF THE NATION, AS OF THE INDIVIDUAL, THAT THE GREATEST DOER MUST ALSO BE A GREAT DREAMER.**
>
> - Theodore Roosevelt

Show Them a Bright Future

A great place to start is with your vision of what things will look like in the future. Regardless of how bad things may be now, you must get a clear vision of how you want things to be. The more vivid you can be with your vision, the easier it will be for others to see what you can see, so make it as colorful and as detailed as you can.

Visualization techniques are a common tool used by NLP (neuro-linguistic programming) practitioners and psychologists around the world. They are used in various areas, but probably the most common place to see their true value is in sports—in particular, golf. The legendary golfer Jack Nicklaus famously said, "I never hit a shot, not even in practice, without having a very sharp, in-focus picture of it in my head."

The reason why visualization is such a powerful tool has been the subject of a number of research studies. Without going into too much detail, the human brain is primarily a visual tool. And while human beings have developed the ability to speak and learn languages, which we use to communicate and describe things, the brain actually focuses on images. Through language, we have created words to describe images, which we then learn and store in our memory.

Imagine you are on vacation in a foreign country, and you are looking for a particular tourist attraction. You can't speak the local language, and the only person you can find does not speak English. It would be very difficult for you to explain to that person what it was you were looking for, and even if you did manage to explain what you were looking for, it would be very difficult for the person to tell you how to get there. But if you had a picture and a map, the language barrier would not be an issue.

For any golfer out there, like me, you will know what it's like to get what you *don't* want even when you tell yourself *not* to do it. A great example of this is when approaching a green that is surrounded by water. You tell yourself confidently you don't want to end up in the water. The green might be ten times larger than the water hazard you are trying to avoid, but nine times out of ten, you still manage to hit the water. The reason is that the brain doesn't understand language, especially not negatives like "don't" or "shouldn't." It focuses on the images or visions you hold in your mind, and because the fear of ending up in the water is so great, that is where you put your focus. Creative visualization is a fantastic tool to help both you and your team reach your goals. The more sensory detail you can put into the vision (how it looks, feels, tastes, sounds, etc.), the better.

As with the example above, when you create your vision for the future, it can sometimes be impossible to remove some of the current problems—or limitations—you face from your mind. You understand your vision needs to focus on what you *do* want and not on what you *don't*, but the mind can often produce the same unwanted pictures in your vision that disturb the positive creative process. The way to get around this situation is to actually bring the fears, problems, and limitations you have into the vision, but now with a *solution* to those fears or problems. For example, say you are nervous about giving a presentation; you fear you will stumble over or forget what you want to say. You might even worry you are going to be sick. In your visualization of the perfect presentation, you would create the scene to play out exactly as you would like it, but then you bring into the mind objections with a phrase like "even though":

"Even though I feel that old, familiar feeling of being sick rising, I take a deep breath and remind myself how passionately I feel about getting my message across and that the sick, nervous feeling is actually excitement. Even though I forget the exact phrase I have rehearsed a thousand times, I breathe deeply, clear my mind, and an even better phrase pops out of my mouth." The idea is that if you are going to have these fears pop up in your mind anyway because you can't always control them, you may as well prepare your mind with a solution in advance. It is a very powerful tool when you integrate your conscious with your unconscious thoughts.

In the previous chapter, I talked about the importance of creating the environment and how, as the leader, you have to be the filter to keep the outside world from getting in. This is especially important when you create your vision because no one will be able to see exactly what you can see, and if you allow negativity in, it could affect the outcome. No matter what people say or do, remember that it's not going to happen overnight and that there may be times when things don't seem to go according to plan. But be consistent with the vision, and you will get there.

Get Your Team's Buy In

While it is important to have a consistent vision, don't feel you have to get everything perfect before you start. As soon as you have a clear image of what it is you want, present it to your team. I suggest the best way to do this is to have a meeting with everyone so you can explain your vision and tell them how long you think it will take to happen.

Depending on how big the vision is and how long you think it will take, you may want to create milestones along the way. These milestones should be believable goals that are realistic and achievable, because if team members do not believe they are achievable, they won't buy into your vision. If you are in charge of people, you likely have a lot more experience than they do, so what is achievable to you may not seem so achievable to your team, but their belief in the vision is crucial.

It helps to hold this meeting somewhere calm and relaxing and to set aside plenty of time for people to ask questions and discuss the vision among themselves. In chapter 3, I spoke about creating a state for learning by making it fun and enjoyable. You will use the same principle here because you want people to be using their creative brains, not their reptilian brains (amygdala). The more you can get them in their creative brains, the easier it will be for them to share your vision and potentially cocreate it with you.

Once you answer any questions and are comfortable that team members can see and believe in the vision, you will want to "future pace." Future pacing is a technique that gets people to visualize themselves having achieved the future goal. It focuses on the "end point." You can do this in a number of ways, but I recommend you get them to express what it feels like to have successfully achieved the vision by using colorful language—words like amazing, wonderful, excellent—to describe how they feel.

Some people will be able to do this faster and more expressively than others, but with a bit of help, everyone can do it. For those who struggle, you can help by asking them questions, drilling down on what it will actually mean to them. Ask them how it will make them feel or see the results on a colleague's face. It can be easier for some people to imagine when they are one step removed. Depending on their upbringing, they may have been conditioned not to show too much emotion or may be distrusting of authority, so you have to create a safe environment where they feel supported enough to express themselves without any fear.

Commit to the Vision as a Team

When you've expressed your vision, got everyone to a point where they can see it, believe it is achievable, and can express what it will be like when they have achieved it, there is a very powerful question you can ask them. The question is based on the R-factor question, created by Dan Sullivan for his DOS conversation workshop, and it goes like this: "If we were all to meet here in three years from today, and you were to look back over those three years, what has to have happened during that period, both personally and professionally, for you to feel happy about what we achieved?"

> **Note**: I use the period of three years because that is what Sullivan used in the original question, but you can use whatever duration of time suits you.

While the question may seem straightforward, it is extremely powerful in that it will answer many of the things you need to know. The first question it answers is, "Do they trust you enough to make this vision a reality?" The second question is, "Do they still want you to be the leader?" If they can't imagine it happening, then they haven't accepted you, and you will want to find out what it is that is stopping them. If, however, they can see themselves three years down the line in a meeting with you, then the answer to both questions is yes, which means they see a future and they trust you.

The second part of the question will help you get a better understanding of what they see as the major challenges to overcome. It also lets you know what they need to accomplish in order for it to be a success. By knowing what's important to them, you know what to include in your plan for making the vision a reality. Every time they achieve one of their goals, that trust and belief in the vision will strengthen.

Another powerful thing this question and the visualization exercise achieves is that it gets people to forget about things that are wrong in

the present and shifts their focus to a future where those problems no longer exist.

Before you end this meeting, make sure you've answered everyone's questions and that you have everybody on board, because if you don't, as soon as they leave the meeting, anyone who hasn't signed up can potentially sow doubt in the rest of the team. However, if you have been following the advice so far in this book, you will know this shouldn't happen, because a) you have nothing to hide from your team, and b) you have their best interests at heart. All of this will have come across when you presented your vision.

I trust you can see just how valuable a process vision building is and why it is so important to spend time to create your vision and plan how you're going to deliver it. Getting everybody on board with the vision will make your life so much easier. When people find themselves getting disheartened with the current state of affairs, you can get them to refocus on the collective vision. This will keep them moving forward.

Create a Solid Team

Team: A number of persons associated in some joint action

Now that everybody knows what you want to collectively create, it's time for your team to build it.

The most effective teams are the ones where every member of the team wants every other member of the team to be successful. Most people will do more for people they care about than they would for themselves.

In the previous section, I suggested you get people to talk about the vision together. Part of the reason for this was not only so they could commit to the vision but also to commit to one another. By doing this, you significantly increase your chance of success because now they have a bigger reason to want to succeed.

From this point forward, your focus will be on creating your team and developing them into a strong, cohesive unit. You want everyone to start taking responsibility and become a leader in their own right.

Remove Rigid Hierarchy

> # LEADERS DON'T CREATE FOLLOWERS; THEY CREATE MORE LEADERS.
> — Tom Peters

In the fourth chapter, I spoke about leadership characteristics and how leaders create leaders, not followers. This is what you should aim to achieve when creating your team.

For many people, this is going to be a lot more difficult than it sounds because giving up control can seem extremely frightening, especially when you are responsible for the outcome.

I have always been very fortunate in this regard because I am an extremely trusting person. I also realized early on that the only way to truly have control is to give it up. The analogy I like to use is that of a pilot. The pilot always takes full responsibility for the people on the airplane, but that doesn't mean they try to control everything that happens. In fact, all the pilot really gets involved in are the actions with the highest potential risk, like take-off and landing or, of course, when something goes wrong. Other than that, the pilot allows everyone else to take responsibility for whatever it is they have agreed to do.

In order to get the maximum out of your team, remove any unnecessary and rigid hierarchy. While I agree that in certain situations there is a need for hierarchy, I think this is generally overused—in some situations to extreme extents.

In my career, I have witnessed this firsthand while working for a company in a country that culturally favors a hierarchal system. The hierarchal approval system was so convoluted that it created numerous bottlenecks that eventually became a real risk to our ability to operate efficiently. Standing outside of the system, I could clearly see simple but effective measures that could completely transform the current processes, reducing this risk, improving efficiency, and—not least of all—saving the company money (in man hours) in the process. Because of the hierarchal system, the powers that be were not willing to change the process because the person who was making the case (me) was not considered important enough. It was nearly impossible to get the parties involved even to meet to discuss it, but those same parties were the ones pushing to get things done in the old, inefficient ways. Perhaps this was an isolated case, and something like this has never happened to you, but if it has, you know exactly why it is important not to let the same thing happen in your team.

For the purpose of this book, hierarchy will not be required, so do whatever you can to remove it, at least during the transition phase.

When I join a new team, I make a point of explaining how things will be from the very beginning. I always come from the perspective that I am starting from scratch. Regardless of how experienced the people in my team are, I don't assume they know what I'm talking about, so I explain everything in great detail. I don't do this to patronize them or to insult them in any way. I do it because I would rather they turn around and say they know, and I don't have to explain it, than to assume they know and get myself frustrated over something I believe they should know but don't. In my mind, it's a sensible thing to do, and I explain *that* to them, too.

I start by showing them an organizational chart synonymous with a typical hierarchal system, with the manager perched on top and everyone else below him.

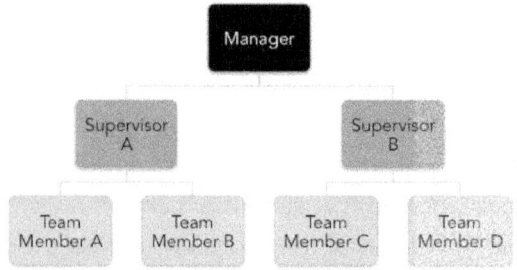

Then I explain my approach and about how I like to manage, which is to see every person as a vital piece of the whole but with different activities and different levels of responsibility.

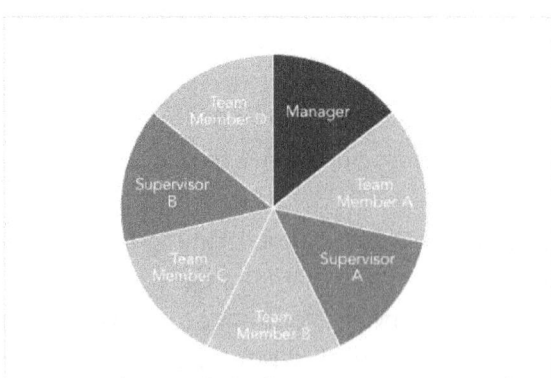

T E A C **U** P

As the most senior person in the department, I assume full responsibility for everything that happens, but like the pilot, I only get involved in the high-risk activities or in instances when my team need assistance, such as advice, guidance, training, or an extra pair of hands.

By taking this approach, I have the freedom to focus on the big picture and to spot any potential challenges before they happen. It also means I am able to see when people are struggling and ensure I'm available should they need me. However, I do make a point of not going to them when I think they need help, choosing rather to let them come to me.

I do this for two reasons. The first is because I want them to know they can come to me any time they want. All too often, people are afraid to ask for help because they think it makes them seem weak, but in my mind, the exact opposite is true. It takes a strong person to ask for help, and I ensure that they know this is my belief.

The second reason is that I want them to know I trust them implicitly. In fact, I trust in their abilities so much that I know that, given the right environment and enough time, they will eventually figure it out themselves. Regardless of whether they need to come to me or anybody else for help, resourcefulness is one of the greatest assets a person can have, and that is what I want to develop in them.

If for whatever reason they choose not to ask for help and subsequently "fail," they have already been assured it's OK to fail and that all they have to do is own their mistake, learn the lesson, and try again. People learn best when they are in charge.

Make Them More than Employees

When you accept a management position, it is my opinion that you accept responsibility to do everything in your power to improve the lives of

The Art of Tea Bag Management

everyone you have the privilege to work with. It's easy to get caught up in the day-to-day grind of work without ever taking the time to step back and really ask yourself what it is you are doing.

Throughout this book, I have spoken about the idea that we are all connected and that by helping someone else, we are actually helping ourselves. In the same vein, if someone else is having a problem, then it's safe to say that we are affected by the same problem. It may not be as obvious or painful for us as it is for the person who is actually going through it, but it will have some effect on our lives.

A common example of this is when someone is involved in an accident on the way home from work. You might not be the one involved in the accident, but there's a good chance the accident will leave you stuck in slow-moving traffic. And what's crazy is that some people actually get angry with the people involved in the accident.

To a lesser extent, there will be occasions when this happens in the office. It may not be an accident, but there will be a time when someone in your team has a personal problem that causes a ripple effect in the office. Getting angry with them will only make matters worse because it will make them more disruptive and put you in a bad mood, too.

The best outcome for everybody would be to face the problem as quickly as possible. Unless you know exactly what the problem is, it's always best to handle it by simply offering to help without going into any detail. Let the colleague know that you are aware something is wrong and that you are available for him or her if and when he or she needs you. This allows your colleague to feel in control and to open up when he or she feels comfortable enough to do so. If you have applied the principles in this book so far, your colleague will know you are being sincere, and when the time is right, he or she will come and see you, so don't feel you have to force it.

T E A C **U** P

I make a point of getting to know all my team members as much as I can, and I want them to know about me. I like to place personal things in the office that have a story behind them—things that are likely to start a conversation about my life and me. I have no issue with telling people whatever they want to hear because it allows them to get a better understanding of who I am as a person. And the more I open up to them, the more likely they will be to open up to me.

The amazing thing about doing this is that once they open up to me, they then start to open up to the other people in the department, too. They stop seeing one another as work colleagues and start to develop deep, personal friendships, making them a strong team. They will look out for one another.

The stronger they become as a team, the harder it becomes for forces outside the department to negatively affect what you are building. This in turn frees up even more of your time, so you can reinvest back into their development.

Bring In the Hired Guns

As you start to put your plan into action and develop your team, you may find the pressure to meet the expectations of the company is too great with your current team. There will be a lot going on for everyone as they try to find their place in this new setup, so the risk of productivity dropping is very real. In fact, I would almost say it is guaranteed in the beginning. I would be more worried if it didn't because that may mean they have chosen to carry on the same way as before.

Pressure is never a good thing, but it is *really* not a good thing when you are making the amount of changes we are talking about. Pressure causes cracks, and cracks make people feel very nervous. If you think this may happen, or if it is already happening, don't be afraid to bring in some hired guns. By hired guns, I mean highly experienced contractors who can come in and immediately handle any pressing issues your department might be facing.

If done correctly, they can play a big part in making your plans a success because they can get to work straightaway, removing some of the pressure caused by day-to-day activities while you focus on setting up your department and developing your current team.

The other benefit of hiring experienced contractors is that they can pass on their vast experience to your team. The quicker you can get your team working at full potential, the quicker you will get the results you're looking for.

It always pays to bring in people whom you already know and who know how you work. They will be invaluable because they can share their experiences of working with you. Third-party praise can be an extremely powerful tool, so bring in people who will support your objectives, and let them help build the team's confidence in you.

It goes without saying that the quality of the people you bring in will have a direct influence on the results you achieve, so be sure to bring in people who align with your goals.

In this section, I discussed what you can do to help create a solid team. Start by removing rigid hierarchal systems that don't add any value. Then, look at how you can make your team members become more than just work colleagues, and get to know each of them personally. Finally, I discussed the benefits of bringing in hired guns to help you through the difficult transition period.

In the next section, I look at development and at how you can help everybody reach his or her full potential.

Make Learning Fun

In chapter 3, I focused on your development and on how important education is in order to become a true leader. In this section of the book, it is time to turn our focus to the development of the team. The quicker you can get everyone on your team to reach their full potential, the quicker you will start to see the results.

We Are Always Learning

Because of the amazing processing power of the human brain, our brains are constantly taking in new information and making new associations—whether we are aware of it or not.

There is a common assumption with humans that we learn by being taught or by reading, but much of what we learn comes from mirroring the people around us. Have you ever caught yourself doing something, a mannerism maybe, that one of your parents is always doing? You swore when you were a child that you didn't want to turn out like your parents, but to your shock and horror, you find you've started doing things they do or did. Don't be too hard on yourself. This is more normal than you might think.

In the animal kingdom, animals learn by mirroring the older members of the group. The experienced animals will often take the younger animals on hunting trips and teach them how to hunt. By observing the adult animals, the young animals are able to pick up the skills they need until they feel confident enough to try hunting for themselves. They then apply what they've learned and adopt a policy of trial and error in which they continue practicing until they have refined their technique and are able to do it successfully on their own.

As humans, we learn in much the same way, except we are not always aware of it. Once you've established yourself as the leader of the team

The Art of Tea Bag Management

and members of the team see you as an authority, their brains become activated to mirror the things that you do—whether you like it or not.

While this may sound a little far-fetched, I can assure you it is true. I found it out by accident while working on an assignment in Africa. I am always on the lookout for new information and for ways I can improve my life. One thing I had uncovered was a crazy-looking pair of shoes called Vibram FiveFingers. They are basically gloves for your feet but have a hard plastic or rubber soul to protect your feet while you're walking. They were originally designed for barefoot runners, but because of the design, they proved to be very good for posture. This is because they allow your feet to sit firmly on the ground in a natural position.

As health is an area where I have a big interest, I started to wear five fingers on a daily basis. I would even wear them into the office, much to the amusement of my fellow colleagues. Because I was reaping the rewards of wearing the shoes, I didn't mind a few jokes at my expense. After a couple of months, the jokes stopped, and people stopped worrying about my wearing them. Then, one day, one of my team members came in to see me and asked me if I could buy him a pair on my next trip home. I of course agreed, and no sooner had I given him his new shoes than the next person came to see me. To cut a long story short, I ended up taking twenty pairs of shoes back into the country in the last year I was on that job. Not once did I try to sell them to anybody or tell anyone to buy them. They saw me wearing them; I told them why I wore them, and that was enough for them to want them, too.

This was a very important lesson for me, because it made me realize just how influential a person can become when his or her peers see him or her as an authority. As a leader of a team of people, you are always passing on information to them, so be aware of the things you do and say.

Time Spent at Work

As mentioned in the previous section, much of our lives are spent in the work environment, so it's important to make sure we make the most of that time. While the main purpose of our going to work is to produce results for the company, we have to be aware of what we are giving up in return for a salary.

In every job, certain results are expected of us, and we must follow certain company rules. In my opinion, it is very possible to both deliver the results expected of us and enjoy being at work while also adhering to the rules of the company. I also believe that not only am I responsible for getting the results that are expected, but I also have an obligation to make the lives of the people who work for me better than they were when I arrived. I want them to value the time they spend at work and not spend the whole day watching the clock until they can walk out the door. That is why I place such a big emphasis on development and getting to know each and every member of the team. When you can get them to start seeing work as somewhere they want to go, then you'll never have to worry about people delivering the results required of them or about their wanting to rush out of the office as soon as it is time to go home.

Have a Clear Development Map for Everyone

One of the most common things I encounter when I take on a new role is people doing a job because they need the money. Their only purpose to come into the office is to do enough for the company to warrant the salary they receive. No more, no less. They have bills. They need money to pay the bills. It's just a dull and depressing cycle that is happening all over the world, every day of the year.

I have a personal quest to break the cycle with every person for whom I am responsible. I want every one of them to have a better reason to come into work than needing to pay the bills, and I do everything in my power to make sure I am successful.

When I first tell people about this, they always ask how many people I have had to get rid of in my career, because they assume they will want to go work somewhere else. In fact, I haven't had a single person want to leave my department once I took over and put into practice the principles I am teaching you in this book.

In chapter 2, I spoke about taking responsibility for our lives and about how important the meaning is that we place on things. I use the same knowledge on each and every one of the people in my teams. I spent time with every single one of them to find out what it is they want from life.

By finding out what it is they want from life, I'm able to help them plot a course that will get them what they want because I believe everyone has the potential to get what they want—if they really want it.

I teach them the key to getting what they want from life comes down to two things: the first is to know where you want to go or the outcome you want, and the second is to know where you are right now. Once you know where it is you are going and where it is you are starting from, people can give you directions to where you want to go.

Depending on where you are starting, getting there might not be easy, but no part of me would ever think it would be impossible. When I sit down with them and explain that what I want more than their just turning up at work and doing a job is for them to reach their goals, they have an immediate change in the meaning they give to work. Whereas before it was a place to come and get money, now it becomes a place where they can get money *and* move closer to their dreams or aspirations.

Just as you created a combined vision for the department at the start of this chapter, you now create individual visions for every member of the team. In addition to creating the vision, you can work on putting plans in place to move them toward their goals.

It is such a powerful transformation to see someone change from being driven solely for money to someone driven by a desire to achieve his or her dreams.

In this chapter, I focused on the team and on what you can do to get them united behind a single vision. You start by creating the vision and presenting it to the team. Getting them to buy into it as a group, as opposed to individuals, ensures that they are driven by the needs of others.

I also looked at ways to create a strong, solid team by committing to their development and being interested in more than just work. Work can be so much more than just picking up a paycheck, but it takes work and dedication on the part of the manager to let the team know they want the team to succeed as individuals as well as the team as a whole.

In the next chapter, I look in detail at some of the development concepts raised in this chapter and see how we can build on the strong team ethic to benefit people outside of the company.

Presence (Just Be)

We have now reached the final part of this book, which focuses on the implementation of the art of tea bag management. I discussed my metaphor of a cup of tea and the three parts that comprise it. In chapter 5, I covered how to create a safe environment, symbolized by the cup, and in chapter 6, I discussed how to unite your team by creating the right environment and culture, symbolized by water. In chapter 7, I focus on you, the leader, symbolized by the tea bag. Once the tea bag is placed in the water, the essence—or flavor—of the tea bag will effortlessly infuse the water in which it is placed. So, too, will *your* presence and "flavor" infuse throughout your department.

> **WITH GREAT POWER COMES GREAT RESPONSIBILITY.**
>
> - Uncle Ben

In part one, I focused on the individual leader and the skills, characteristics, and attributes of leaders. In this final chapter, you will see why it is so important to master them and do whatever you can to continually develop your leadership skills.

As the responsible person, you will be seen as the authority whether you like it or not, and it is up to you how you choose to use that power and influence. In this chapter, I refer back to a number of principles and concepts I have already covered, but my hope is while the content may be the same, the context in which they are being delivered will have changed because of the understanding you now have of how it all fits together—allowing you to make valuable new insights.

Every Move You Make

In previous chapters, I discussed learning and about how animals learn by mirroring their parents and elders. Your team will constantly be mirroring the things you do and say because you are the responsible party. When I try to explain this to people in my courses, I get them to imagine a pond. Around the edge of the pond, there are thousands of stones and pebbles of all different sizes. I then get them to imagine picking up a stone and tossing it into the pond. Regardless of the stone's size, a ripple effect spreads out across the entire pond. The water itself doesn't actually move; it is just the up-and-down movement of the water caused by the stone entering the water.

The same thing happens with you and your team. If you react to something in a very animated and aggressive way, it is like a large stone dropping into the water, sending stronger ripples out across the pond. Your challenge as a manager is to try to minimize the amount of ripples in the pond.

I think is important to note at this point that, while your actions will have an effect, it is every individual's responsibility to choose how he or she reacts to your actions. People's ability to react is dependent on how conscious they are of whatever it is that is affecting them. Much of what we are being influenced by is coming to us subconsciously without our even realizing it, and that is what we need to be aware of.

As an example, imagine sitting in your office with your team around you. You start to get little hot, so you want to turn the air conditioning up. You now have two choices: you can turn the air conditioning up without asking anybody and hope nobody notices, or you can ask them if they mind your turning up the air conditioning. If you chose not to ask them, then they would start to feel the cold but would probably not be aware of why, and, potentially, they would just carry on working as normal, just a little colder. On the other hand, if you did ask them, they would be aware of how your actions will affect them, giving them the choice of how they wish to respond.

This happens all the time and is prevalent in teams where the managers avoid having any interaction with the people. The people are disengaged and probably spend the majority of their day in a trance.

If you look at this from a negative context, it may seem all doom and gloom, but these same principles work in a positive context. Remember that, as the leader, you are the tea bag, and whatever flavor you choose will infuse those around you.

Start Observing

To start using this principle, the first thing you need to do is observe. Try to step outside of yourself to get a perspective of everything and everyone, almost like being a spectator watching a sports event. By stepping back and observing, you become much more aware of everything that is happening. It's too easy to get caught up in the detail and lose sight of the bigger picture.

This won't happen overnight and is going to take practice, but the effort will definitely pay off. Create reminders that go off at certain times during the day that remind you to take five or ten minutes just to observe.

When you first start doing this, it is best to do so silently to try to avoid getting into trivial conversations with people. You'll also need to do it in a way that doesn't arouse too much suspicion.

Initially, it may raise some eyebrows, especially if you are used to spending the entire day locked in your office, but the more you do it, the more normal it will seem for everybody. If people do question you, don't be afraid to tell them what you're doing. We've already discussed the importance of being open, so here's a great chance for you to start. There are other benefits too, including the following:

* Shows them your vulnerable side because you are going out of your comfort zone to make things better
* Lets them know you are interested in them
* Increases their trust in you because you are acting on your promise to them

Get Their View

Average people spend most of their time looking at the world through their own eyes, which is completely normal. I can only speak for myself here, but I can't recall any of my teachers explaining the importance of perspectives and how what *we* see and think the world is, is not necessarily how *other* people see it. We are so conditioned by the dualistic view that we are separate from everything around us that we unconsciously live our lives looking outward. Very rarely do we stop to find out what it's like from the other side.

One of the few TV shows I like to watch is *Undercover Boss*. It is a reality show that follows CEOs of companies as they go undercover, doing various different jobs in their own company. By going undercover, the CEOs get to work with the people and find out what it is like to work at the company from the people's perspective. By becoming a coworker, the people tell them things they would never normally hear. This is an extremely powerful process, and I've yet to see an episode where a CEO was not moved and inspired by the personal stories.

When we put ourselves in these ivory towers to show off our importance, we lose our connection to the people, and we also lose sight of what is important to them. While I agree that sometimes you do need to visit the ivory towers to get a higher-level view, I don't think you need to stay there all the time. You should spend the majority of time on the ground floor with the masses.

Throughout my career, I've always made a point of getting to know everybody's names, from the cleaners all the way up to the very top. I always take time to talk to them or at least greet them no matter what. I treat them all as people, regardless of their roles. If they choose not to respond, I don't take it personally, and the next time I see them, I greet them again.

Because I am like this with everybody, others quickly learn that that is who I am and that it is not contrived. I am not doing it for any gain; I do it because I believe it is the right thing to do. This kind of openness allows me to connect with people on a personal level and makes people feel open enough to tell me things they wouldn't normally tell their bosses. I use these relationships to get feedback from them, which helps me move forward and improve things that are not working well. I also ask them to give me personal feedback so that I can constantly improve myself to be the best I can be.

The idea of getting feedback, especially personal feedback, still scares me to this day, but I do it because I know it will help me improve. I'd much rather people say it to my face than walk around thinking everything is fine and have people talk about me behind my back. The caveat to that is that sometimes the feedback may actually be someone else projecting onto me, and I have to recognize when that is the case. Always

make a point of only using feedback you think will benefit you, and don't take everything on as being gospel. If you get the same feedback a number of times, it's probably worth looking into.

Be the Change

> **IF WE COULD CHANGE OURSELVES, THE TENDENCIES IN THE WORLD WOULD ALSO CHANGE. AS A MAN CHANGES HIS OWN NATURE, SO DOES THE ATTITUDE OF THE WORLD CHANGE TOWARDS HIM**
>
> - Ghandi

Now that you have had a chance to observe things from a new perspective and receive feedback from your team, you should have a good idea of where you are and what needs to be done. That may seem like a contradiction, especially considering this chapter is not so much about doing but rather about being.

Most of us have grown up with the idea that in order to be something, we first have to do something, and by doing something, we then achieve some results, and then because we have the results, it means that we are what we wanted to be. This is known as "do, have, be."

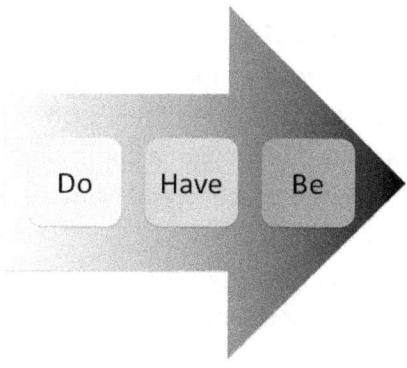

The Art of Tea Bag Management

So if I wanted to create a united team in the office, I would first have to do something, whatever that may be. By doing this thing, we would then achieve some results. Once we had the results we were looking for, that would then make us a united team.

While some may argue that this is how things work, I believe it happens slightly differently. I believe in the approach made popular by Zig Ziglar that goes "be, do, have."

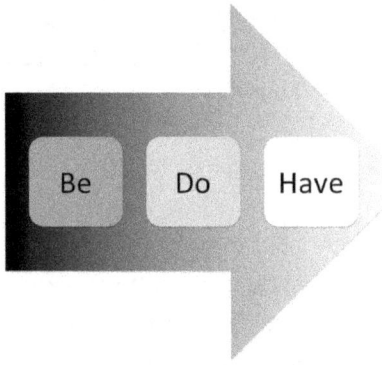

While both approaches seem very similar, there is one major difference that ties in to chapter 2 and the principle of taking responsibility. The first model suggests that we are a consequence of our actions and that the actions we take make us who we are. However, we know this is not true; it's who we are that determines the actions we take and, therefore, the outcomes we achieve.

This tiny distinction can make a massive difference to your success in applying the principles in this book. In order to make it work, you have to "be" first. In that, I mean you have to "be," whether it's physically or mentally, with simply your belief of a united team with a common vision—regardless of whether you have achieved the results you want.

If people start to criticize your approach or your team, you have to ignore the negativity and remain united. Remember, you are in control.

Stay focused on the end game, and don't allow the naysayers to destroy the vision you are creating. Be what you want.

Good People, Not Good Employees

Now that we understand more about how the infusion happens and about the mind-set you need to make it work, I will focus on having the confidence to let things develop naturally.

Monitor and Track

By now, you should have a good understanding of the art of tea bag management. You will understand why just by being in that environment affects everyone and everything in the environment. For many people, the most difficult part of the whole process is in letting go and trusting it will work. We've been conditioned to believe we have to be doing something and that to achieve things takes hard work and dedication. I, too, believe in hard work and dedication—but only when it is required.

If you are building a department from scratch, then you will probably have a lot more going on and will very likely be extremely busy trying to juggle all the different elements of setting up the department and applying these principles. On the plus side, though, you will have the advantage of it all being new, so you won't have to undo any bad habits. It is also easier to get people to believe in the vision because it is a new group of people without existing grievances or resentments.

A great way to visualize this is by imagining a spider's web. During the construction of the spider web, the spider is extremely busy putting everything in place and getting everything organized. Once the web is completed, the spider's job becomes much less hands-on as it simply monitors, maintains, and attends to any disruptions within the web. This is how I see the manager's role: to constantly monitor and maintain the environment and to deal with any external "influences" that threaten the stability of the team.

For some people, the urge to be "busy" may seem too great. We are conditioned into thinking not being busy means we aren't being productive, and people may have an issue with it. We want people to like us, so there is a great urge to want to be seen doing something. Again, this is looking at it from an individual perspective without considering the whole. You need to have time on your hands to be able to monitor what your team is doing—not from a controlling perspective, but with a view to make improvements that benefit everyone.

Leaders Not Followers

If the idea of giving up control sends shivers down your spine, what I'm about to say may push you over the edge. Previously in this book, I discussed the idea that great leaders create other leaders, not followers. It is an idea I live my life by and one that is at the forefront of my mind in everything I do. I want to pass on as much of my knowledge as I can to benefit future generations. So as you free up more and more of your time, it's time to start passing on some responsibilities and creating leaders.

As a leader, you know you can't do everything yourself and that in order to really thrive you will need help. Earlier I discussed "be, do, and have" and the idea that, in order to achieve something, the first step is to be the type of person who has what we want to have. If your goal is to create leaders, you start by letting them be leaders. Just like the leaky jug analogy, you have to give them more and more responsibility until they reach a problem. And once they hit the threshold (start to leak), you guide them through it so they can develop.

I don't want you to think this is just an easy opportunity to pass on all your work and responsibility to others so you can sit back and put your feet up. On the contrary, this is a critical point in the development of your team, both for all the individuals and for the department as a whole. While you may be passing on responsibilities, you still have the ultimate responsibility for everything that happens in your *area* of responsibility, so the buck still stops with you.

You also have to support them by letting them know you are there for them whenever they need you. Sit down with them individually and discuss your plans. Let them know your vision for them, and get their buy in; you want them to believe it's achievable. If they can believe it, they can start to be it. Find out if they are happy to do it and if they have any concerns. Make sure you give them full reassurance that you will support them and remain responsible.

By now, you should have had enough time with everyone in your department to know what their development plan is. You will also know what they want to get out of life on a personal level, so the kinds of roles and responsibilities you pass on should ideally be ones that benefit them. If you explain to them why it is you are giving these responsibilities to them, they should accept them with open arms.

Getting them to believe in the vision of who they can be is a critical step, so keep an eye on them. Doubt will inevitably creep in, so you will want to constantly reassure and support them by reminding them of the vision and expressing your confidence in their abilities. People live up to the expectations of those whom they look up to. So let others know you have high expectations for them, and don't show concern when things aren't going well.

Return to the Fire

When I talk to people about the art of tea bag management and I explain my metaphor, they grasp the concept fairly quickly. But while

The Art of Tea Bag Management

the concept is quite easy to grasp, the implementation can be extremely challenging on a physical, emotional, and energetic level. This depends on each individual and how far along a person is on his or her journey.

When I set off on my journey of discovery, I had completely selfish intentions. When I knelt at the bottom of my bed with my laptop open in front of me, I had no intention of ever writing a book. In fact, all I really wanted was some relief from the pain I was feeling. By typing the question into Google and hitting enter, it opened the door to my own amazing adventure, which I grabbed with both hands.

With every step I took, my belief in who I was and what I could achieve changed, increasing my passion for life and my self-esteem. Every time I attended a new training or a self-development seminar, I had this renewed energy and vitality that kept me going forward, because the energy and support I got from other like-minded people helped remove the doubts that constantly crept into my mind.

The best way to explain it is to imagine a burning campfire. If I pick up a piece of wood and place it on the fire, then the wood will start to burn like the rest of the wood on the fire. But if I remove the piece of wood from the fire and place it on the ground, then the flames will eventually die out; the wood will not burn on its own. All I have to do, though, is pick up the wood and place it back in the fire, and it will start to burn again.

While the art of tea bag management is about creating happy and productive teams in a work environment, it is also very much a personal journey. Along the way, there will be times when you start to doubt yourself or doubt whether this will ever work. There will be many demands on you mentally, emotionally, and energetically, so make sure you return to the fire whenever you have to.

TEACUP

Live a Full Life

> **THERE IS NO PASSION TO BE FOUND IN PLAYING SMALL, IN SETTLING FOR A LIFE THAT IS LESS THAN THE ONE YOU ARE CAPABLE OF LIVING**
>
> - Nelson Mandela

While growing up in South Africa during the apartheid years, my view of what was happening in that country was being manipulated by the pro-government media and educational system, all of which were designed to only feed us information that promoted the cause of the government.

In 1989, I returned to Britain to see family and travel around Europe. The flight tickets were a reward given to me by my parents for finishing high school, which I had finished in December of the previous year. I had been in South Africa since I was five and had only returned to Britain once before, when my grandfather died, so this was a big trip for me. It was the first time I had ever traveled alone, and having left England at such a young age, I didn't really know my extended family that well.

I arrived in Britain at the peak of the demonstrations and pressure against the South African government to end apartheid and to release Nelson Mandela from prison. I had no idea Nelson Mandela had become the main icon for the anti-apartheid movement. In fact, I knew very little about Nelson Mandela. In school, I had been told he was a terrorist who had been caught trying to blow up a train station and who was sent to Robben Island prison. It was all very matter-of-fact and seemed to be a sensible thing. Needless to say, I was involved in a number of heated debates about the political situation in South Africa during that vacation—so much so that I eventually started telling people I was from Zimbabwe just to avoid the constant barrage of aggression.

The Art of Tea Bag Management

When I look back now, it seems so long ago. I have learned so much more about the apartheid struggle, and Nelson Mandela is one of my most-admired role models. The most obvious change for me is who I am now compared to who I was back then. I knew very little about the world and had extremely low self-esteem, but now I live such a wonderful, colorful life and have so many new skills. I have traveled to many countries and met lots of interesting and amazing people whom I now call friends. I really do feel privileged and grateful.

It is my humble opinion that to inspire people, you have to live a full life—whatever that may be for you. People want you to show them that, no matter where they come from or who they are, they can make their dreams come true. Hundreds of thousands of stories tell of people who have overcome some of the most challenging circumstances to achieve unbelievable feats. Even if you haven't achieved all that you want from life, the fact that you are willing to put yourself out there and go for it is enough to inspire others.

Remember, you are the tea bag in this metaphor, so the person you are and the flavor you bring will be what infuses the department. Walk your own path; take full responsibility for your life; lead by example.

www.ingramcontent.com/pod-product-compliance
Lightning Source LLC
Chambersburg PA
CBHW061441180526
45170CB00004B/1505